Praise

'*Dare to C.A.R.E.* is a well-written book looking at the intricacies of the customer experience in the times we live in, intertwined with the author's own holistic personal journey, experience of life coaching and work in hospitality. With clear case study examples from the cruise ship industry, amongst others, it shows how these principles are relevant for any business. The author demonstrates how businesses can stay one step ahead of the game through use of the human touch and genuine connections. Carmen's C.A.R.E. model is a spiritual approach to business transformation for individuals, teams and organisations.'

— **Monica Or, MA, FIH, MCIPD** – The Dancing Hotel Inspector, Founder of Star Quality Hospitality Consultancy, award-winning Hospitality Consultant, Amazon best-selling Author, Trainer, Hotel Judge and International Keynote Speaker

'*Dare to C.A.R.E.* is a step-by-step guide for the type of business transformation and personal growth journey that will inspire you to make the difference you were born to make. We all have the ability to create a better future for ourselves and those around us, and each one of Carmen's chapters provides the guidance we need to evolve and transform to become the best version of ourselves and powerfully impact the world around us. Make it your personal and professional growth handbook.'

> — **David Carruthers, MBA**, Business Strategist, Mentor and Coach, Keynote Speaker, Founder of Future of Hospitality, Grow My Hospitality Business and David Carruthers Consulting

'The book takes us through different experiences, from the individual level to the organisational level. Even if we refer to the business and the goals of creating experiences for customers, it is obvious that mental preparation, education, self-awareness, authenticity, development as an individual in spiritual and professional terms are indeed the cornerstones to achieve these goals. In this sense, the C.A.R.E. Model can help to better understand this transformational approach at an individual or group level.'

> — **Professor Dr Gabriela Țigu**, Dean of the Faculty of Business and Tourism, Bucharest University of Economic Studies (ASE)

'In a crowded field of business and self-help books, *Dare to C.A.R.E.* stands out for its innovative approach to merging customer-centric strategies with personal well-being. The author shares her perspectives and expertly guides readers on how to tackle challenges and overcome the complexities of life. Her writing is engaging and accessible, making it easy for readers to apply her wisdom to their own lives. Combining practical wisdom with an inspiring vision, the book defines a clear path to achieving sustainable growth and enhancing the human experience. If you are a business leader, aspiring manager, student or someone looking to thrive in today's demanding world, this book delivers a transformational roadmap to success and well-being.'

— **Adam Rowledge MBA, CMgr, FCMI, FHEA,** Managing Director Rowledge Associates, Keynote Speaker, Lecturer Anglia Ruskin University, University of Sunderland and University of Buckingham

'*Dare to C.A.R.E.* is a powerful and transformative guide that merges personal growth with organisational and/or professional excellence. Through the innovative C.A.R.E. Model, the book empowers individuals and businesses to navigate uncertainty, cultivate genuine connections and foster resilience. Drawing from years of expertise in hospitality and leadership, it offers actionable insights for aligning personal well-being with professional success. With its unique blend of real-life examples and visionary strategies, this book inspires readers to redefine their purpose and drive meaningful change in every aspect of their lives. A must-read for thriving in a rapidly evolving world.'

> — **Ovidiu Folcuț**, Full Professor, VP of the Romanian-American University Senate, Member of SOREC (Romanian Society of Economics), Editorial Board Member of the Romanian Economic and Business Review, IETI Transactions on Data Analysis and Forecasting, Research Focus Journal

'Carmen has poured the depths of her heart into this project. You will not only read the words, but you will also feel her passion as you read. If you want to grow in your personal and professional life, your overall well-being, and also your approach to customer service, then do not hesitate to get your copy today. I highly recommend it!'

> — **Steve Wormer**, Minister, The Memphis Church, Executive Director of Hurt to Hope, Amazon best-selling Author, Leadership and Life Coach and Keynote Speaker

Dare to C.A.R.E.

UNLOCK YOUR POTENTIAL TO TRANSFORM YOUR LIFE, WELL-BEING AND CUSTOMER EXPERIENCE

CARMEN F. VLASCEANU PhD

Re think

First published in Great Britain in 2025 by Rethink Press
(www.rethinkpress.com)

© Copyright Carmen F. Vlasceanu PhD.

I stand humbled and grateful to God, who guided me along my journey to transform this book from a dream into reality.

This book is dedicated to my beloved son Adam, your presence in my life has been the compass steering me through the seas of challenges and joys. Your unwavering support and love are the gifts that enhance my life and inspire my actions.

To all my family and friends scattered across the globe, your support has been a source of inspiration and encouragement transcending the world's borders.

With heartfelt appreciation,

Contents

Foreword

Hospitality is a people-driven industry and as CEO of the Institute of Hospitality and a lifelong participant in the dynamic world of hospitality, I have witnessed firsthand the transformational potential of people-focused leadership.

Most issues across the hospitality industry and other sectors who strive for customer excellence are rarely just logistical. The solutions all boil down to educating, understanding, motivating, and empowering people.

The *Dare To C.A.R.E.* model is a blueprint for 'Connection, Authenticity, Re-engineering and Evolution,' and addresses both personal and professional dimensions of success.

This holistic approach resonates deeply in hospitality, an industry where human interaction is irreplaceable, adaptability has become a non-negotiable skill and where elevating the customer experience is a necessity

The author's emphasis on professional and personal growth as a cornerstone of exceptional customer experience is particularly compelling. Many books have been written on leadership, customer experience and personal development, but *Dare To C.A.R.E.* bridges the gap between these topics by providing insightful advice for individuals and leaders to enhance their emotional intelligence and create a more empathetic workplace culture.

The book encourages each of us to impact on our communities by acknowledging the importance of empathy in our lives and striving to build stronger relationships not just with our family, friends, employees, and customers, but everyone around us.

The hospitality sector operates in an increasingly volatile environment where people and leaders are constantly required to pivot and innovate due to the rapid technological advancements, shifting customer expectations and global disruptions. But amid these changes, one truth remains constant: the value of authentic connections. It is in this context that *Dare To C.A.R.E.* delivers its greatest strength, offering practical tools and actionable strategies while reaffirming the importance of leading with empathy, integrity, and vision.

The sections dedicated to enhancing customer experience offer profound insights into how businesses can create lasting impressions and foster loyalty, transforming customers into advocates.

The chapter on re-engineering your mindset offers an interesting perspective on navigating change, complete with real-world examples and insights that will resonate with readers across industries.

The focus on customer experience as a pivotal aspect of well-being and professional success underscores how interconnected our roles as leaders, individuals and service providers truly are.

Similarly, the sections on building authentic customer connections provide a guideline for fostering collaboration, trust, and service excellence – three cornerstones of any successful organisation.

Dare To C.A.R.E. is a guide that challenges its readers to look inward before they lead outward. It encourages the reader to reflect on your own life journey through **C**onnection, **A**uthenticity, **R**e-engineering and **E**volution, while offering practical tools to cultivate these traits in others.

My professional connection to the author has allowed me to witness her unwavering commitment to personal development and her profound understanding of the human element in business. As someone who is personally invested in nurturing the next generation of hospitality leaders, I admire the author's ability to translate complex challenges into simple, actionable steps. Her work, both in this book and in the broader scope of her career, reflects an inspired blend of wisdom and accessibility.

The are many benefits to reading the book: for young talent and seasoned professionals, it provides a fresh perspective to build skills and confidence to enhance their impact within organisations, and for everyone else, it serves as a reminder that life is a journey, not a destination; one that requires continuous learning, reflection and personal transformation.

As you turn these pages, prepare to be inspired, and encouraged, as *Dare To C.A.R.E.* is a call to action for everyone who aspires to make a meaningful difference in their teams, organisations, and communities. Its perspective on life, well-being and customer experience is transformative and timely and I encourage you to embrace its principles, apply its insights and share its wisdom with others.

Whether you are a hospitality professional, an aspiring leader, or simply someone committed to personal growth and achieving customer excellence, this book will undoubtedly leave a lasting impact. I am confident that, like me, you will find its message both inspiring and transformative.

Robert Richardson FIH MI,
CEO, Institute of Hospitality

Introduction

*D*are To C.A.R.E. is intended to be your guide in learning the art of **C**onnection, **A**uthenticity, **R**e-engineering and **E**volution in both your personal and professional life, in a time when it has become harder to distinguish between the two. This book gives a comprehensive strategy for prospering in a world full of uncertainty and complexity, regardless of whether you are an individual looking to accomplish personal growth or a business looking to improve customer experiences. Drawing from decades of my practical expertise in global hospitality, business management and life coaching, *Dare To C.A.R.E.* offers a thorough framework that synchronises individual growth with organisational transformation.

You will discover how to better prepare to face life's uncertainties with confidence and perseverance, how to overcome personal obstacles and break free from limiting beliefs through the personal case studies that appear throughout the book, drawn from my real-world experiences and some of my tried-and-true personal empowerment tactics.

In the business sphere, *Dare To C.A.R.E.* provides company leaders and their teams with valuable insights on how to cultivate a culture of empathy and growth to attain organisational excellence and improve customer experiences.

Directly addressing matters relating to individual personal development to learn how to create meaningful connections with the customers, actually benefits the organisations, helping them build more resilient teams that are empowered to implement transformative strategies to drive sustainable success.

The C.A.R.E. Model bridges the gap between personal aspirations and professional demands, creating a synergistic approach: by aligning these two facets of life, people will enhance their well-being while contributing to the growth and success of the organisations they work in.

Dare To C.A.R.E. begins zooming in on the customer experience, which is the cornerstone of any successful business. It provides valuable insights into the teams' collaboration in the functional context of organisations. The spotlight, however, emphasises how each individual (the smallest unit of our society) holds the key to making a profound difference. It is through this inward journey that the book explores the critical elements of excellence that link customer experience with individual well-being.

As the narrative progresses, it becomes clear that true power lies within each individual to foster personal growth and well-being and dramatically influence our organisations, as well as the broader society around us. Each of us, at some point, plays the dual role of both a provider and a consumer of products and services. This means that our actions and decisions ripple out-wards, contributing to the enrichment of the human experience on a global scale.

Why does this book matter now? In our world today, it has become increasingly tough to maintain the balance between personal well-being and professional success. In order to address this challenge head on, I designed the C.A.R.E. strategy to provide some practical tools that could be implemented in everyday routines to help you successfully master the difficulties of modern life. The model aims to position the book as a handy solution for both organisations and individuals in the pursuit of excellence in both personal and profes-sional areas of life. I must admit that hospitality holds a special place in my heart. To me, it goes beyond a welcoming spirit and a smiling face, to encompass opening doors for those in need and showing kindness to strangers. Hospitality is the best industry to work in, allowing us the chance to make lasting memories with every conversation and every encounter. Whether it is organising events, creating delicious meals or making guests feel truly at home, these are all opportunities to demonstrate the power of genuine care. Hospitality is simply my true passion, and it has been the vehicle by which I manifest my love for people.

But the challenge of hospitality, also known as the 'industry of smiles' – and, in a broader context, of providing a positive customer experience in whatever line of business we might be in – is that we may not always feel like smiling ourselves.

Presenting a warm and responsive face to our customers means we often have to draw deep on our personal resources, which can leave us feeling drained and demoralised. All too often I have seen the strain that maintaining a sunny public persona can place on an overstretched individual.

So, how can we develop a state of well-being that helps us and enhances our ability to take care of our customers?

Whether you are a hospitality professional in one of the many branches of this beautiful industry or an entrepreneur building a new business, the capacity to interact with your customers in a way that leaves them wanting more is essential. I have been embracing all the challenges the hospitality industry has to offer for over thirty years, starting with junior jobs in local

hotels, moving to a stint in aviation catering, and culminating in the role of a senior officer in charge of the
guest services department aboard cruise ships carrying
over 5,000 passengers – where I have literally seen it
all, from marriage ceremonies to a man overboard and
even murder.

All customers have their own peculiarities, but cruise
ship guests are among the most demanding in the
world! To begin with, they have paid a large amount
of money, often for the journey of a lifetime, and are
therefore entitled to expect a seamlessly uplifting experience. Then, of course, for a large part of the time they
are in the middle of the ocean, and there is no escape,
no alternative, if things go wrong. And sometimes they
will go wrong, for unavoidable reasons such as poor
weather or crowding at ports, or entirely avoidable ones,
such as overeating and too much sun! The scope for dis-
appointment is limitless. At such times, the hospitality
professionals will have to dig deep to give of their best.

We know from our own personal involvement as
consumers how dramatically our expectations have
changed over the past decades, and we need to extrapo-
late from that how likely they will change in the future.

In Part 1 of the book, I will present an overview of what
customer experience means for consumers, organisations, teams and each individual. History has shown
how strong an individual can be and that we must
never underestimate the power of one.

Having witnessed firsthand the challenges of providing a rich customer experience, from the minutiae of day-to-day life on board a cruise ship to negotiating the intricacies of hospitality at international tourism fairs, to undertaking life coaching sessions with my clients, I've come to understand just how strong the need is for a foundation of resilience and inspiration in order to make it in the world. I accept that perhaps I am not a typical author, but I am a versatile individual whose life experiences, professional journey and academic discipline have converged to bring you a book that is as perceptive as it is authentic and insightful. This broad range of exposures has given me an insight into the whole landscape of customer experience and the human state of happiness and well-being.

The continuous constraints of everyday life might make us feel overwhelmed as we try to balance many competing duties. As time passes and the challenges keep coming, we may become less willing or able to perform to the best of our ability and consistently provide great service to those around us. In the heap of obligations and constant expectations, it is easy to lose sight of our aspirations and the vibrant energy that once fuelled our lives.

For me, when times were tough, my love for people and my passion for the hospitality industry guided and motivated me to improve my skills, see things differently, and build strength. With each challenge, I saw a way to show my dedication and a chance to think about and change what living with purpose means for me.

If you're looking for inspiration and a fresh connection to your dreams, this book is here to help you feel confident as you face uncertain times. We will explore different strategies and real-life examples to help you develop a positive mindset that will prepare you to handle challenges and come out on top. I am committed to helping you develop the inner power to turn adversity into success.

I have developed the C.A.R.E. Model to structure this approach, and in Part 2, we will be analysing each of the following four elements in more detail:

- Connection: A deep communion with the divine, with yourself, with nature and with others develops your capacity for empathy and understanding.

- Authenticity: This is a vital factor, helping to identify your passion and purpose in life and direct your efforts as you move forward.

- Re-engineering: Constantly adapting your perceptions and reframing your responses through tools is key for shifting your mindset and embracing positivity and growth.

- Evolution: With every obstacle you overcome, and as your resilience consequently increases and your mindset is refocused, you will become more inspired and you will find the creative energy to continually recalibrate your course.

In a spirit of openness, I must declare that a strong connection with the divine and my personal Christian faith has guided me to become more focused and better equipped to navigate the complexities of life. I accept that many people do not share this faith, but I think that each one of us believes in a higher governance, and what we do share is a common desire to give of our best and strengthen our ties with our inner self and those around us. We are all brothers and sisters, and we are more alike than we generally like to admit. The essence of *Dare To C.A.R.E.* stems from my desire to see as many people as possible rediscover the unbreakable confidence in their potential and produce results to achieve their dreams.

Dare To C.A.R.E. is written as a tool for this mindset shift: it encourages you to reassess your objectives, redefine your purpose and align your actions with a profound sense of meaning. Consider the book as a source of inspiration, bringing you closer to the manifestation of your boldest dreams. As you read on, imagine a renewed sense of purpose crystallising within you. I encourage you to see your true self, feel strong enough to act, set clear goals and stay focused on what matters to you. Join me on this trip where *Dare To C.A.R.E.* will serve as your roadmap, steering you toward personal achievement and business development success.

PART ONE
EXPERIENTIAL LIFESTYLE

The experiential lifestyle has become a popular way for people to prioritise their well-being and happiness, and in recent years, improvements in technology have made products and services significantly better. The experience economy, as explained by Pine and Gilmore (2013), is about building a culture that focuses on having special and unforgettable experiences instead of just owning things. This means people are paying more attention to taking care of themselves, being aware of their thoughts and feelings, and working on improving themselves as they look for happiness and purpose in their lives. People are now more aware of their mental and emotional health and they look for interesting things to do that help them grow and learn about themselves. The modern consumer wants to live more thoughtfully and to connect better with the natural environment, and because of this, business organisations are implementing environmentally conscious strategies focused on sustainable practices and customer experience, to stand out and create strong bonds with their audience.

1

A Journey Into Customer Experience

In our first chapter, we will explore the captivating world of customer experience (CX) and learn what truly sets a business apart in today's world of commerce and connectivity, where products and services are abundant. The quality of products and the efficiency of service has been overtaken by the consumer's expectation of a more holistic encounter, the customer's journey from the moment they become aware of a need to the point of fulfilling it. Customer experience refers to the intricate network of encounters, perceptions and expectations the modern consumer has when dealing with businesses. In this first chapter, we look at the heart of customer experience, dissecting its complexity and underlining its significance in today's experience-driven economy.

Introduction

For many years, the currency of trade has meant moments of joy, relationships made and memories produced, rather than being reduced merely to dollars and cents changing hands. The present is defined by an undeniable tendency towards rapid change and innovation, especially in the field of technology, where advancements evolve at an unprecedented rate compared to any other age in history. Every interaction is therefore an opportunity to enchant, engage and leave a lasting impression. The landscape of consumer behaviour, organisational strategy and the transformative power of exceptional service makes up the heart and soul of the contemporary experiential economy.

The power of customer experience

Customer experience is the driving force behind every encounter, and is the fundamental pillar upon which businesses build their empires. The dynamic environment of modern commerce, in which the multitude of options reduces the attention span, has favoured the growth of CX as a critical driver of success. Imagine yourself having an experience where you enjoy each moment, appreciate the personalised treatment you are being offered, and have a positive overall sense of well-being. We must consider all of the aspects of a customer's interaction with a business to truly understand why CX is crucial. Besides providing a product or service, organisations aim their focus on generating memorable experiences that trigger emotional responses from customers. Every encounter has an impact on the customer's experience, from the initial contact, throughout each step of the journey, and ending with the post-purchase assistance. Understanding these subtleties is critical for brands looking to compete in today's market, which is centred on the quality of these experiences. It makes us feel good when the barista at our favourite coffee shop recognises our name, or when a website is simple to use and understands our needs, and, when things go wrong, it is helpful to have prompt and courteous assistance from customer service.

Imagine you enter a neighbourhood bookstore, where the familiar scent of paper and ink takes you to a familiar place dear to your heart. Recognising you, while you look at the books, one of the store assistants comes to ask if you need any help, suggesting books that might be of interest to you. In this small interaction, the assistant has managed to turn a simple bookstore visit into a pleasant encounter, making you happy to come back.

The same scenario, of taking the time to serve with grace and love for people, can also be transposed to everyday life and across all industries, retail, hospitality, healthcare, education, and in this way the world can become a nicer place to live.

Irrespective of whether you are ordering a morning latte, booking a vacation or having a medical appointment, CX shapes every interaction you have, filling it either with fulfilment or, on the contrary, frustration, in the case of unmet expectations caused by a low-level of service. Let's consider some examples of how CX helps create loyalty through enjoyable experiences that strongly connect customers to brands: an online retailer which streamlines the checkout process, minimising friction and maximising convenience, or a luxury hotel that anticipates your preferences, from pillow firmness to room temperature, creating personalised comfort, or the cruise line that welcomes you aboard the ship with a chilled bottle of champagne and chocolate covered strawberries in your cabin celebrating your upcoming birthday. Digging deeper, what are the key determinants of CX? Let's look at what separates an exceptional experience from just a regular, forgettable one.

To begin with, communication is essential, and connects every interaction like a strong thread. Talking clearly and kindly builds trust and understanding, which helps create strong connections. Convenience is vital because it makes things easy for customers, which can mean smooth shopping across different platforms, easy returns, or fast delivery. Convenience turns services into happy and easy experiences.

Personalisation makes experiences richer by turning general interactions into special ones in a way that feel more personal to you. Customers want personalised suggestions and services that match their individual tastes and identities.

Let's not forget how important it is to also assist customers even after they buy something. Good customer service comes to the rescue when things go wrong. When support is quick and caring, it can change a bad experience into a good one, making customers more loyal even when there are problems.

In simple terms, CX is the art of delighting customers at every turn, going beyond what they expect to create memorable experiences. It's about making connections, not just making sales, and creating a group of loyal supporters who share your brand with others.

As businesses adapt to the changing world of trade, CX stays the same: it is not just a strategy, but more like a way of thinking, a mindset. It means we focus on the customer in everything we do. The CX concept can be adopted in both our professional and personal lives, and, if implemented correctly, the results will be visible and impactful, replicating positive outcomes in various aspects of our interactions and relationships. Think about this: right now, every one of us is involved in a service, either in the sense that we are a customer, or we are providing a service to someone else. From this perspective, it may be fairly considered that the world revolves around serving, and whether it is giving or receiving service, it must be done candidly, with a genuine desire to help others and make a positive difference.

Without service, our society would not function efficiently. This is why it is critically important to recognise the value it provides and appreciate those who provide it, in order to successfully replicate a harmonious and cooperative community. This can also serve as a motivating factor for others to do the same, to contribute with their effort and time for the benefit of society. This changing role we all share – of being both service providers and service customers – shows how important it is to understand and address the needs and expectations of both sides to better prepare and succeed in the experience-based economy.

On the other hand, at an individual level it is important to realise that each of us are in the position to make a difference in the lives of others and help create thriving communities by simply being kind and showing empathy in our various job roles and in every other interaction. It is the little things that make up the big picture.

To better grasp the implications, let's consider the example of a sales assistant who, for the past few years, has been working at a grocery store where Dr Jenny usually purchases her food supplies. Every day, the sales assistant consistently makes an effort to be friendly to Dr Jenny and exchange some positive energy, but on one particular day, the sales assistant's mum needed to be urgently taken to the hospital for a critical procedure. Dr Jenny, who was working at the time, quickly stepped in and reassured the sales assistant that everything possible would be done for her mum, touching her heart. Here, *excellent customer experience is the outcome of a genuine and humble human experience for both Dr Jenny and the sales assistant*. It can truly change lives with every interaction, in the same way that taking the time to listen to a friend in need can have a significant impact on their well-being.

It is your turn to treat others how you want to be treated. You might want to offer a helping hand to someone, or simply share some of your time or your gifted talents.

My dear reader, we have now seen how demonstrating compassion and empathy towards others truly holds the power to significantly transform everyone's lives, and you, too, can make a difference.

Sailing into excellence: Cruise customer experience

For the past decades, the cruise industry has established itself as a major force in the global hospitality environment. Providing the greatest degree of hospitality excellence, the majestic floating hotels have been navigating the world's oceans offering an unrivalled blend of luxury, comfort and adventure. As a thriving sector of global tourism, the cruise industry has experienced exponential growth over the past thirty years, serving as a benchmark for transformational maritime experiences. At the heart of this exceptional industry is the concept of cruise customer experience (CCX), as described in one of my previous research articles (2024) – an exceptional blend of quality hospitality services and innovation.

Navigating the oceans year-round, cruise guests explore the world's natural beauty, from the clear turquoise waters of the Caribbean to the magnificent fjords of Norway and Alaska, while indulging in local traditional cultures. Aboard majestic cruise ships, your every need is anticipated and the experience is designed to offer a seamless service. The concept of cruise customer experience is nothing but a cohesive journey that transforms the ordinary into the extraordinary.

Personally, I love this floating world of hospitality, having worked for over a decade as one of the senior officers aboard various cruise vessels. What sets the cruise industry apart is its unwavering commitment to delivering exceptional experiences at every touchpoint. Every interaction is meticulously designed to delight and astonish, from the moment customers initiate their online cruise search, looking to book their next vacation destination, to their actual cruise journey on one of the majestic ships, and onto the final farewell at debarkation, culminating with their extended stay in one of the cruise city ports on their trip home. You step onto the deck of a glamorous cruise ship and are greeted by the friendly crew members, and as you walk around the ship in awe and admiration, you feel surrounded by comfort and luxury and set for an unforgettable voyage.

Working in the guest services department of cruise ships provides a unique perspective into the world of customer experience. Nowadays, cruise ships have a capacity of 5,000–7,000 guests, and, depending on the length of the voyage, every week or every few days, depending on the length of the cruise, thousands of new people embark and the only constant that remains unchanged is the service excellence.

Given the extremely high turnover, as you might imagine, there could be all kinds of situations that arise, and so patience, empathy and quick critical thinking are crucial to ensure optimal resolution and to provide the much-desired memorable experience to every customer. Above all, it requires a tremendous love for people. All the people, regardless of ethnicity, gender or background.

I'd like to give you a glimpse into the highs and lows of working in this high-turnover environment, and this particular instance involved a guest who was unhappy with their accommodation. He stormed over to the purser's office demanding an upgrade and, disregarding his fellow guests and the pursers working at the front desk, he asked to speak with the manager. The purser listened attentively to his concerns and tried to reassure him that everything possible would be done to find a solution to make his stay on board enjoyable.

Hearing that, he became even more aggravated, shouting and demanding to speak to a manager. Shortly after, I was called to step in and meet with the guest. I introduced myself and explained that the ship's cabin allocation is pre-assigned and that his booking records had to be investigated to establish what had actually happened at the time of reservation. I reassured him that the matter was going to be looked into and I went on to further investigate. It wasn't long until I approached him again, and, sitting down at one of the coffee tables, I calmly explained to him that it appeared a misunderstanding had occurred and a lower category of cabin had been booked than the one he had originally intended. By then, the guest had calmed down, and was addressing me by name, asking what could be done. I took the time to explain that the ship was fully booked and that the embarkation process was currently ongoing, and that there was no telling at that particular time whether one of the other guests might not show up. He was assured that he would be contacted later on that day as only after the ship's departure from port would it be possible to know whether a more suitable cabin had become available by then. The guest gained a full understanding of the situation and left, thanking me for taking the time to explain and stating that he would speak to his travel agent when he returned home. Later that day, he was contacted and offered a room upgrade that had become available due to a no-show, and the guest felt satisfied and valued. There have, of course, been other instances when offering a cabin upgrade has not been possible due to the capacity constraints, but establishing a personal connection with an angry or disappointed guest, and communicating with empathy, will always help defuse conflict, making a big difference to their experience.

Even though the guest in this case exhibited disagreeable behaviour, the composed demeanour of the purser and the manager, coupled with respect and professionalism, led to a positive outcome. Ultimately, he left the purser's office, appreciative of the outstanding customer service he received and feeling remorseful about his earlier harsh demeanour.

Without a sound experience strategy, organisations will struggle to retain consumers and maintain a competitive edge in the marketplace. Improving the customer experience is a vital component of success in every business sector. Initially, with our angry guest, the crucial component was to pay close attention to his comments and concerns, and provide alternative possibilities and reassurance. This helped pinpoint the important issues and enhance the guest's overall experience.

Here's another example that shows how important human experience is to customer experience: a special moment when we organised a surprise birthday party for a guest with specific medical needs. Along with the guest's family, we secretly decorated the room with balloons, ordered a lovely cake and a member of staff dressed as a superhero character to help brighten the atmosphere. This fun surprise made the guest feel special and appreciated; her smiling face made all the hard work feel worthwhile and we felt that our initiative and creativity to find the appropriate solutions truly made the guest and her entire family happy, which is the most important aspect of working in the hospitality industry.

What is essential in all of this is wanting to make a difference in someone's life, to always act in good faith, and times like these make working in the hospitality industry truly rewarding. If we always try to exceed people's expectations, we can create special memories for our guests and improve their overall experience. In the end, it's the strong commitment to giving great service that makes successful hospitality workers different from the rest. This comes from a real love for people. Doing extra things and being creative can really help make special memories for the guests.

This is true and applicable to both our professional and our personal lives. It is the satisfaction of knowing that we have given one hundred percent to make a positive impact upon someone's experience that makes all the effort worthwhile.

The pinnacle of customer experience excellence

Think of customer experience as an elaborate staircase, with each step representing a unique tier of involvement and fulfilment, much like Maslow's hierarchy of needs. Maslow's theory posits that human needs are arranged in a hierarchy of importance, and that individuals must fulfil their basic needs before they are able to seek higher-level needs such as belonging, self-esteem and self-actualisation.

CX includes everything, from the most basic elements of service, to forming deep emotional connections involving many types of interactions, and this range of ideas makes us think differently about how we see customer relationships and what loyalty really means. At the most basic level, companies need to make sure that their products and services meet the fundamental needs and expectations of their customers. Ascending further up the ladder of CX, we reach the emotional realm of connections and belonging. Here, brands go beyond meeting the customer's simple needs, and begin fulfilling their wider desires, evoking emotions and forging deep bonds with their client. Finally, high above, right at the top of the ladder, we find transformational CX, the holy grail of customer centricity. Here, the differentiating factor is being able to spark changes, to inspire growth and create memories that last a lifetime.

Understanding and strategically navigating these echelons is a matter of utmost importance for businesses if they are to elevate their CX efforts to new heights. Many organisations around the world have reached the top level of customer experience, leading the way for others. In today's tough business world, where competition is strong and customers want more, many leaders in the hospitality industry have excelled in the customer experience they provide. They are change catalysts, creating new standards and inspiring others with their impressive ideas and changing the way we all think about service. Their success comes from a strong dedication to being the best at what they do. From fancy hotels to cruise ships and cosy bed and breakfasts, these leaders know that taking care of guests is more than just providing service, it is a chance to create real connections and happy moments for them. Their leadership in CX is evident in everything they do, from implementing new techniques to improve customer experiences, to using technology and information to understand what their guests want and need. They are always finding new ways to make things better, creating seamless booking platforms, helpful concierge services and smooth operational processes.

What makes these leading organisations different? For starters, they are setting new standards and encouraging others to do the same; they are dedicated to doing excellent work and being creative in experience design, which helps them stay on top in the global market. They realise that customer experience is not just a single department's job, but a way of thinking that affects everything within the company, from the front desk to the back office, and every employee is properly trained and encouraged to provide great service to create unforgettable moments for the customers. The amazing numbers show how successful they are; they have the best guest satisfaction ratings and high occupancy rates. These leading organisations are always better positioned than their competitors by providing great experiences that go beyond what people expect and continually focus to build loyalty.

We all know that the best proof of CX leadership is none other than the customers' stories, those who have experienced the service themselves. It is not a secret that the organisations whose focus is on providing a great experience for guests manage to build a loyal group of customers. This loyalty helps them thrive over time, and good recommendations from customers and repeat business are not just signs of success, they are essential for a sustainable business.

The echelons of CX serve as guiding lights as the business landscape continues to evolve and customer expectations continue to rise, illuminating the path forward for those who seek to excel in service and innovation. Understanding the echelons of CX therefore becomes essential for businesses seeking to elevate their customer interactions from mundane to memorable, from satisfactory to sublime. Brands can craft experiences that resonate with customers on a profound level, driving loyalty and sustainable success, by strategically navigating these levels. The leading organisations inspire admiration and model excellence, shaping the future of their industry using the timeless principles of hospitality and service.

CX business design

Business organisations from various fields have been successfully replicating CX models inspired by the hospitality industry. Over the past few years, we have all noticed how companies in the healthcare industry, manufacturing, transportation, e-commerce, education, communication, banking and entertainment, all came up with creative ways to attract and make us happy. After all, it is well known that a good service provided turns regular situations into special ones by exceeding people's needs before they have expressed them, and doing more than what is expected brings benefits in the long run. From a CX perspective, not all encounters are created equal, and Net Promoter Score (NPS) is a widely used metric in customer experience programmes that helps assess customer loyalty based on their propensity to recommend a business. Understanding the echelons of CX is essential for businesses seeking to orchestrate memorable experiences that resonate with their customers long after their journey with you ends.

CX has evolved over the last two decades from being a mere consideration to being a vital strategic initiative, and the technological advancements that have come along have changed the way customers engage with brands on multiple platforms, forcing businesses to adjust their marketing strategies in order to maintain market relevance. The modern customer's expectations are varied and continuously changing, as they are frequently performing extensive research before finalising their buying choices. Progressive organisations understand that CX extends beyond marketing and customer service; it influences all aspects of the business, including product development and the overall corporate culture and business mentality. And so, to improve effectiveness and create synergies with customers, one needs to organise business operations around the CX principles and successfully engage and resonate with one's target audience by carefully studying the various backgrounds and demographics that influence their preferences and behaviours.

Just like you and me, customers around the world have developed their ability to recognise seamless omnichannel experiences and prefer proactive problem-solving and customer-centric organisations that cultivate lasting relationships. Nowadays, people look for organisations who prioritise convenience, consistency and personalised interactions across all touchpoints, and this shift in consumer behaviour determines transparency and authenticity in operations and marketing strategies. In a world where competition is harsh and differentiation is difficult to achieve, organisations must shift from a product-centric to a customer-centric approach, putting

CX at the centre of their operations. However, this is rather challenging without a thorough understanding of the people they are trying to reach. Recognising the emotional and psychological variables that influence consumer behaviour is critical for building meaningful relationships and providing excellent customer experiences. A firm built around CX stresses empathy, responsiveness and authenticity in all interactions. This commitment to authentic connection can set a company apart in a world where superficial interactions are becoming the norm.

Can this be achieved in an increasingly shallow society that lives in fast forward mode? Besides selling products or services, the spotlight should be focused on solving problems, addressing needs and creating value at every touchpoint. And how can that be achieved with the high employee turnover rate which occurred from the pandemic years onwards? It is not an easy undertaking and, in part, the answer lies in training, either internal or external learning and development programmes, created to equip employees with effective tools and empower them with crisis-resolution skills focused on elevating the human experience of the customers.

The goal should be about removing barriers, anticipating needs and exceeding expectations in ways that delight and inspire repeat business encounters. From the architectural decor design of hospitality establishments and venues, to the layout of digital interfaces or the personalisation of customer services and attention to detail, every aspect needs to be carefully crafted to provide a memorable and enjoyable experience for guests.

As Peter Fader and Sarah Toms highlight in *The Customer Centricity Playbook*, businesses who prioritise CX are more resilient in the face of adversity and also more proficient at capturing long-term value and fostering sustainable growth. Aligning strategies, processes and culture around the needs and desires of their customers enables businesses to create a virtuous cycle of loyalty, advocacy and profitability that propels them to new heights of success.

Business Transformation 5.0

We live in times of uncertainty, where change is the only constant. The concept of Business Transformation 5.0 refers to organisations seeking to thrive in the digital age. This transformative journey is characterised by a fusion of AI, innovation, customer centricity and a continuous pursuit of excellence. In addition to maintaining their relevance, today's businesses are striving to take the initiative, influencing future trends and reimagining the boundaries of possibility. At the core of Business Transformation 5.0 is the understanding that thriving in the modern market demands significant and transformative change. There is no limit to what can be done with AI transforming all facets of business using predictive analytics to foresee customer demands. AI is fundamentally altering our operational methods, our communication and our interpersonal connections, and businesses are increasingly adopting it as a key driver of innovation to stimulate growth.

However, innovation by itself is insufficient, and Business Transformation 5.0 demands a profound comprehension of fundamental customer desires and preferences, alongside an unwavering dedication to ongoing enhancement. This customer-centric approach ensures that innovation is both creative and strategic in driving business transformation. Successful companies rely on feedback to adjust their products and services and enhance their processes to surpass previous experiences and expectations. Staying relevant is a transformative process that requires constant adaptation and evolution; it is no longer sufficient to just meet customer needs, one must anticipate their preferences and get in position one step ahead of the game, offering solutions in accordance with emerging trends. Business Transformation 5.0 stirs up agility and responsiveness, being attuned to the ever-changing markets and customer preferences. It is essential to embrace change as a catalyst for growth, to seize opportunities as they arise and position oneself for long-term success in an increasingly competitive environment. Just as in any other aspect of our lives, mindset is everything, and we must embrace change as an opportunity to innovate, not see it as a threat. Only those who succeed in doing so will challenge conventions to differentiate and lead, pioneering new paths forward.

Summary

As we come to the end of this chapter, let us remember the core of CX, understand its complexities and recognise it as a key business concept. We have explored how this strategy highlights the human aspect in our business relationships, placing the client at the centre of all our initiatives; from foundational principles to the importance of emotional connections, we have acknowledged the critical role that CX plays in promoting exceptional encounters and developing long-term partnerships.

Further, we have explored the world of cruise customer experience, where luxury and great service create magical and unforgettable holidays. Inspired by the principles of hospitality, other industries have embraced sophisticated CX strategies, recognising their potential to improve engagement and create lasting memories. We then talked about CX design, where empathy, responsiveness and authenticity take centre stage in every interaction. We learned that by aligning strategies, processes and culture around the needs of customers, businesses create a synergy cycle of loyalty and profitability. Finally, we've concluded that by embracing change as a catalyst for growth and innovation, businesses are in a better position to thrive, delight their customers, inspire their employees and drive sustainable success.

2
Organisations

In Chapter 2, let's continue to analyse the world of experiential economy, customer experience and how one person can truly make an impact. This chapter looks at how businesses operate. It focuses on what makes them successful and how their culture and leadership mould the brand and guide their strategies, and we will examine how organisations work and how people within them can create change.

Leadership

Any successful organisation relies on leadership to bring together inspiring and motivating individuals, setting a vision and guiding the team towards achieving that vision. Effective leaders actively demonstrate the power of example, 'walking the talk' and embodying the values and goals of the organisation (Northouse, 2018) with their strong decision-making skills, adaptability and ability to navigate any challenges that arise.

It all begins with a vision; a leader must have a clear idea of where they want to take the organisation and be able to communicate it effectively to the team. The vision motivates employees to work towards common goals, providing a sense of direction and purpose. Great leaders have strong interpersonal skills that help them build relationships based on trust and respect – essential for creating a positive work environment. Empathy and active listening play significant roles here, and understanding the needs and concerns of the team members is crucial in making sound and well-informed decisions.

Another vital aspect of leadership is adaptability, as the business landscape is constantly changing. It is important to navigate these changes effectively on both professional and personal levels. The key traits of effective leadership along with a series of intangible characteristics specific to the business environment can also be applied in everyday life at an individual level. This requires an intrinsic willingness to learn and grow, as well as the ability to remain calm under pressure. Effective leaders know how to delegate and understand that they cannot do everything by themselves, and empowering team members and entrusting them with responsibilities increases efficiency when training future leaders within the organisation. Perhaps some of us fondly remember that supervisor or manager who left a strong impression on us, who successfully managed a multicultural team, creating a friendly atmosphere in the office and encouraging open communication. That leader whose open-door policy and ability to connect with team members from various cultures and backgrounds, understanding their unique perspectives and integrating their ideas into the organisational strategy, exemplifies effective leadership. By taking this approach, that supervisor managed to drive productivity while creating a supportive work environment where the individuals felt valued and empowered.

Authority

Exercising authority through decision-making, policy adoption and implementing changes for the benefit of the team and organisation is essential. Let's take the example of a manager who inspires trust, respect and collaboration by using his authority to implement a new policy aimed at improving workflow efficiency. Because it directly affects the employees, he first talks to them, gathering feedback and listening to their concerns and suggestions. Instead of just imposing this change, his approach ensures a smoother implementation and better outcomes. Notice how important it is to balance authority with empathy and have a good understanding and ability to maintain trust and respect among team members (Goleman, Boyatzis and McKee, 2013).

Now let us consider a different example, this time of a manager who lacks authority – this was one of the clients enrolled in my personal development counselling sessions. She was a mid-career professional working in a corporate environment who was facing challenges with showing her authority and communicating assertively. She was highly competent and respected by her peers, but she struggled to assert herself in meetings and decision-making situations. She often kept quiet even when she had valuable insights to offer. Her lack of confidence and assertive communication skills were holding her back from fully participating in her role and causing her to miss many opportunities for career advancement, and she had a growing sense of frustration. In our one-to-one meetings, we focused on developing her communication skills, particularly in expressing her thoughts and ideas confidently and respectfully, using techniques for assertive communication, including 'I' statements and active listening, practising these skills through role-playing exercises. She was encouraged to start slowly by expressing herself in low-stakes situations before gradually moving on to more challenging interactions. We also worked on building her self-esteem, addressing the internal barriers that were contributing to her reluctance to speak up and act boldly in certain situations. Over time, she became more comfortable, expressing herself more forcefully but empathetically in the workplace and she began to display authority by delegating more and contributing actively in meetings. It was not long until her input was recognised and valued by her colleagues and superiors. In the end, her confidence grew and her job satisfaction increased, and as her authority increased, she moved forward and took on new opportunities for leadership within the organisation.

Authority should not be confused with authoritarianism. Leaders who express their authority without empathy are at risk of creating a toxic work environment, triggering reductions in morale and productivity. Effective leaders use their authority to guide with a sense of fairness and empathy, to create structure and order within the organisation by setting clear expectations and accountability. This type of authority is constructive and is used to empower employees rather than to control them. Leaders who effectively balance authority with empathy create a more positive work environment; they are approachable and open to feedback, which helps in building trust within their team. Trust is crucial because it encourages open communication and fosters a collaborative atmosphere; when employees feel that their leaders understand and respect them, they are more engaged and motivated to give their best.

Authority, when exercised with respect and regard for the human experience, drives positive change and innovation within the organisation. And while decisions are being made efficiently, the human element should never be overlooked, thus also maintaining a balance that promotes productivity, employee satisfaction and well-being.

Organisational culture

The values, beliefs and norms shared among employees is often referred to as organisational culture and it has an important role in the internal environment of a company (Schein, 2010). We all appreciate working in a company that encourages employee engagement and open communication, favouring creativity and boosting overall performance. Let's pause for a minute and remember how you might have felt in your first professional undertaking. Perhaps you were lucky, like me, to be part of a company whose culture was creating a sense of community, where people were collaborating genuinely and helping each other. This sense of belonging can only be achieved through team-building activities, open communication and an inclusive environment where diverse perspectives are valued and all the people are respected.

From my personal experience, the cruise industry offers a unique organisational culture and a multicultural environment with people from all over the world. Depending on the size of the ship, imagine hundreds or thousands of crew members from various cultural backgrounds living and working in close quarters for many months at a time, interacting with a few thousand guests from all around the world, representing almost all the nations of the world. This diversity undoubtedly enriches the organisational culture, fostering a sense of community and mutual respect which enhances the overall cruise guest's experience, as discussed by Guzzo, Fink, King, Tonidandel and Landis (2014).

A strong organisational culture generally results in a higher level of innovation, encouraging employees to feel free in expressing their ideas and come up with creative solutions. This type of environment is often seen in the leading organisations in various industries. It is the efficient blend of leadership and thriving organisational culture which allows them to stay ahead of the competition and continue to improve and adapt to the new challenges.

CASE STUDY: Multiculturality in the cruise industry

Let us return for a moment to the unique organisational culture of the cruise industry, where crew members interact with thousands of guests from all over the world while living and working aboard the majestic mega liners for months at a time. Going down memory lane, I remember experiencing all kinds of challenges. As a senior officer responsible for guest services and customer experience, I regularly dealt with problems. I had to think quickly and find creative solutions to keep our guests happy. It was a tough but worthwhile experience that taught me important lessons about being flexible, solving problems and communicating well when things are stressful. I encourage young hospitality professionals to consider working on a cruise ship, as the experience acquired is incredible and may lead to many great opportunities in the hospitality industry. While it might be tough at times, exposure to different conditions broadens one's perspective and aids in the development of a global perspective as well as the capacity to perform efficiently under pressure.

I recall one day a Hispanic guest who did not speak English was looking for her missing child and, after searching for some time without success, the mother approached a crew member who was carrying a tray of drinks on the lido deck. The crew member immediately showed empathy, trying to understand the distraught mother, and quickly looked for another crew member who spoke Spanish, and then directed her to the purser's office to report her missing child. Upon hearing these directions, she left in a rush and shortly after she got lost and was unable to find the purser's office. Her evident preoccupation for the missing child's whereabouts, coupled with the language barrier, prevented her from remembering the directions she was given. However, one of the two crew members' quick thinking and compassionate response, taking her personally to the lower deck, helped her report her missing child. When she got to the purser's office, the international staff were easily able to find someone who spoke her language. They worked together to find her missing son by getting in touch with all the right departments and starting a search of the ship. The mother started to feel less worried when she saw how hard the team was working to help her find her child. A message was sent through the ship's intercom telling all passengers and crew to help look for the missing child.

Later on, after an intensive search, they were able to locate the five-year-old boy near the pool area, who was also looking for his mum. The family was safely reunited and the mum expressed her immense relief and gratitude for the quickly organised response of everyone involved.

This incident highlights the value of diversity and cooperation, as demonstrated by the crew members' ability to effectively communicate and work together in a crisis situation. Without consulting with a supervisor, the crew member instantly took the decision to escort the guest to the purser's office for further assistance. This expression of empowerment and the swift exercise of authority and decision-making, ultimately led to a successful resolution of the crisis at hand – a perfect example of how priceless it is to create an inclusive environment where all team members feel empowered to contribute their unique perspectives and expertise. Working on cruise ships truly provides a firsthand insight into the intricate dynamics of a multicultural environment. The employees navigate customer service challenges and cultural differences daily, contributing to a cohesive work environment that enhances the guest's experience. Such everyday interactions underscore the importance of teamwork and empathy and a genuine care for the customer's humanity. It brings up how diverse perspectives and skills contribute to personal and professional growth, fostering a supportive environment that benefits both employees and guests (Hofstede, 2001). In this instance, the quick thinking and cultural awareness of the crew members turned a potentially distressing situation into a positive experience for the guest.

These types of interactions also highlight the significance of training and development when creating a positive, thriving organisational culture. Crew members aboard ships are regularly trained in cultural sensitivity alongside customer service, which equips them with the skills needed to handle diverse situations effectively. The training, which is continuous, not only enhances their professional skills but also promotes personal growth, making them more adaptable and empathetic individuals. The multicultural nature of the cruise industry is a microcosm of the globalised world in which we live, and it should be more often regarded as a successful example to follow in all our organisations. Effective communication across cultural boundaries is essential. We should all celebrate our differences, as we can all benefit from a large spectrum of abilities and a diverse range of experiences and talents, enhancing our collaboration and relationships with our colleagues and our customers.

All business organisations aspire to succeed and begin their operations with the end in mind. It is no secret that it takes a lot of hard work and dedication to achieve a high level of recognition in any domain. But what does it actually mean for different organisations, and how do we measure success?

Organisational success is linked to achieving specific goals, and Kaplan and Norton (1996) introduced the concept of the Balanced Scorecard as a performance metric, arguing that success includes financial targets, reputation, internal processes, learning and growth. It is an efficient tool that helps business enterprises track performance across various operational dimensions and align their strategic objectives with key performance indicators. In order to achieve long-term sustainable success, it is worth thinking about what success actually means to you and your organisation, and begin building from there.

Re-engineering

Tough times always bring out the best in us, although change is always difficult. Remember what we all experienced during the Covid-19 pandemic and how we had to find inner strength and determination to get through it? Some of us had to make enormous changes to our lives to get used to the new situation. Just as everything else around us, the business world is constantly changing, and just as in personal life, companies need a great deal of flexibility to adapt. Often, they have to change their processes and think about how to operate differently. Re-engineering processes, adjusting costs, introducing new technologies, or reorganising departments could be just what the company needs to stay profitable. The goal is to achieve dramatic improvements in critical areas such as cost, quality, service and speed, and nowadays artificial intelligence is employed to automate routine tasks, freeing up employees to focus on more strategic initiatives. This re-engineering effort sets the tone for a mentality of continuous improvement among employees and promotes a culture of innovation. Hammer and Champy (2009) highlight in their research that re-engineering processes and systems helps increase efficiency and drive innovation within an organisation.

The tourism industry was severely impacted by the travel restrictions imposed by governments around the world in response to the Covid-19 pandemic, and it had no choice but to somehow find a way to survive. The dramatic outbreak had a profound and extensive impact on the entire world, affecting the well-being, financial stability and way of life for billions of people. All of a sudden, the crisis became a significant threat to the global economy, disrupting all the industry sectors in ways that have proven difficult to reverse. For businesses, this meant that they had to suddenly evaluate, re-engineer their business models and introduce contingency plans and crisis management protocols to ensure the continuity of their activity.

Let's look again at the cruise industry, which was forced to abruptly halt all the operations on a global scale for more than a year, and more than almost any other tourism sector, it suffered severe losses and a dramatic decline due to the border closures. The industry may well have struggled for many years following the pandemic, if it was not for its agility and ability to pivot and quickly re-evaluate and re-engineer their business models. For instance, to maintain financial stability, cruise operators were compelled to liquidate assets, including many of their older ships. The industry had to adopt pioneering strategies to start sailing again, while prioritising customer safety and well-being. This re-engineering process redirected the focus towards promoting domestic tourism and exploiting local markets to sustain business activities. Despite the significant challenges posed by the pandemic, the cruise industry demonstrated remarkable resilience, adapting to the constantly evolving travel restrictions and eventually restarting cruise operations amid significant uncertainty (Vlasceanu and Țigu, 2021).

Business environment vs life

There are some moments in life when we realise that our greatest asset is our mindset. The process of re-engineering pushes boundaries, forces a shift in mindset, challenges the status quo and transforms the way we think and act. This is easier said than done, especially having to let go of limiting beliefs or established practices to embrace the unknown. It starts with being open to new ways of doing things, and this is as true in our personal lives as it is in business. Have you noticed how we are instinctively drawn to those who have a growth mindset and inspire us with their ability to learn from setbacks and emerge even stronger than before? We tend to feel the same about a company with a story of success, a business that managed to overcome challenges and be reborn from its ashes. Sometimes, being in a vulnerable position and having the strength to recalibrate our thinking ignites incredible growth and success. The benefits can be substantial, including increased efficiency, better personal relationships or customer service, an improved level of confidence and a stronger competitive position. A successful re-engineering effort, whether in life or in business, is about shifting the perspective, improving communication and building strong relationships. For instance, a good manager works closely with employees, knowing that the reasons for upcoming changes and how they will benefit them and the organisation need to be explained. Leaders must be committed to the process and provide the necessary resources and support to ensure that changes are accepted, and that there is a smooth transition to the new norm.

Just as in business, on a personal level we must also constantly adapt, learn and evolve to succeed in a rapidly changing world (Senge, 2006). We need to be open to learning every day, and we need to embrace the discomfort that comes with pushing ourselves out of our comfort zone. Keep in mind that not all the strategies we adopt will be successful, but this should not discourage us from being willing to embrace new ideas and keep moving forward.

CASE STUDY: Resistance to change

A common theme encountered often in one-to-one personal development counselling sessions is the steadfast reluctance some people have to trying new experiences. After digging deep into the core of this resistance, it often stems from a fear of failure or the unknown. One of my clients, a young entrepreneur, was battling with a constant fear of failure that was hindering his business growth. After several sessions of introspection, he discovered an inner struggle with low self-esteem and self-doubt, and one of the ways we found to combat this was to familiarise him with the power of visualisation and positive affirmations. Despite having the skills and knowledge, his negative self-talk and fear of rejection was holding him back. His constant negative self-perception and fear of failure were resulting in missed opportunities and a lack of confidence in pursuing his goals. Using visualisation techniques, he adopted a new perspective imagining himself successfully achieving his business goals and overcoming all the challenges ahead of him. We worked on crafting personalised affirmations to directly address his fears and self-doubt, which he would repeat daily to reinforce a positive mindset. Over time, these practices helped him rewire his thought patterns, reducing anxiety and increasing his confidence to take on new challenges. After a while, he felt more likely to act without thinking of failure. This new confidence translated into success and he began to implement new strategies in his business.

As we can see, re-engineering can be extended to personal development as well and, just as businesses continuously improve their processes, we must also strive to grow and become the best we can be in our personal lives, too. This cannot be achieved without thorough introspection to identify our native gifts and talents, and then drawing from those, the courage to pursue our dreams. Embracing change and being open to new experiences leads to greater fulfilment and success in all aspects of life (Argyris, 1991), and this applies to both personal and professional growth, allowing us to develop new skills that will help us succeed in everything that we do.

In both business and life, we should look at success as a journey, not as a destination, and we must overcome our setbacks and keep going. We owe it to ourselves to have the courage to act, adopt a growth mindset and allow ourselves to evolve and achieve our full potential, both in business and in our personal lives.

Summary

This chapter has looked at the key elements of effective organisations, such as leadership, authority and organisational culture. We have explored how these factors contribute to economic success, as well as the significance of balancing authority and empathy. Using the case study taken from my time in the cruise industry, we witnessed the importance of intercultural relations and collaboration and what a big difference a small act can make. We also discussed the need to re-engineer our processes for continual improvement. At the end of the chapter, the comparison between business and life was emphasised, highlighting the importance of adaptability and proactive growth in both. A clear understanding of the complexities of the modern experiential economy will be useful for both individuals and organisations wishing to adopt a more innovative and growth-oriented mindset.

3
Teams

This chapter takes us into the dynamic world of the teams within our organisations. Just as the family is the basic cell of society, employees are the heartbeat of any business. Their role is crucial in achieving organisational goals and creating a sense of belonging to a community. A good team is a lot more than just a group of people working together, it is a connected unit where teamwork and common goals make great things happen. In this chapter, we will investigate different perspectives about the nature and function of teams, including the problems they deal with. Come along as we explore what teamwork is all about and what helps it succeed.

Challenges of the work context

It is no secret that working within a team context presents its own set of challenges. One of these is handling the complex dynamics in teams that bring together a mix of people with diverse backgrounds, skills and personalities, which can sometimes lead to misunderstandings and conflicts. Effective communication is key to overcoming these challenges and it is important to create an environment in which all the team members feel comfortable expressing their ideas and concerns. This favours the development of healthy relationships where the team members can resolve conflicts between themselves and enhance collaboration (Tuckman, 1965).

Particularly challenging is effectively managing conflicting priorities. Perhaps, like me, you have also come across instances where you and your team had different opinions on which tasks to prioritise and which tasks could be delayed for a later time. I don't know how it was in your team's case, but in mine, such disagreements caused tension among us. In fact, I would be lying if I did not admit that conflicting priorities actually decreased the department's productivity. It is fair to say that it is essential for a team leader or a manager in charge to set clear goals and priorities, ensuring that everyone in the team is on the same page and that the right course of action is followed. Regular meetings and clear communication help the employees work better together and reduce problems caused by different priorities. It's important to deal with conflicting priorities early on by creating an open conversation and letting team members share their concerns. It is also good to create a system for the team members to solve problems that may arise between them to keep the team strong and everyone happy.

Dealing with constant change and uncertainty is a big challenge. I remember when working on cruise ships how rapidly our tasks were altered and how we were constantly undergoing quick training sessions, in addition to the high employee turnover rates. It is therefore imperative for team members to have the ability to adapt and handle changes easily. In her book *Mindset: The new psychology of success*, Carol Dweck (2006) explains how important it is to provide training and tools to help team members build these skills.

One way to eliminate these problems is to build trust and friendship among team members. Trust is the basis of any human relationship. When team members trust each other, they work together better, share ideas and help one another. Gaining trust takes time and requires everyone within the team, both the leaders and members, to work together. Lencioni (2002) highlights that team-building activities, communicating freely and celebrating accomplishments can strengthen bonds between colleagues building better teams.

CASE STUDY: Fire onboard

Allow me to share another real-life experience that highlights the importance of teamwork and resilience in a crisis. During one of the cruise-ship voyages I worked on, we were cruising the beautiful Alaskan fjords when we were faced with an unexpected and dangerous situation, the kind that everyone fears: fire on board. It was a regular evening and the ship was bustling with guests enjoying their dinner when the fire alarm started to disrupt the joyful atmosphere. The fire broke out in one of the many kitchen areas and the situation could have quickly escalated into a full-blown disaster, if it had not been for the sharp senses and quick response of a crew member who happened to be there at the very moment smoke began billowing from the kitchen, and he instantly started fighting the fire. Immediately, other crew members jumped into action, each one knowing exactly what to do thanks to their rigorous weekly training and drills which, quite frankly, everyone disliked. Shortly after, the emergency response team also showed up and started evacuating crew members to safe areas while others focused on containing the fire.

The coordination, knowledge and quick action and all the crew members coming together to help out made all the difference, from the incipient stage of the incident until the end. They helped turn a potentially disastrous situation into a successful firefighting operation. An important aspect of this incident was the calm and composed demeanour of the crew member who noticed the fire at the very beginning. Despite the danger and the chaos created in the kitchen, he remained focused on the task of containing the fire. Crisis management and communication were key in this instance. Expertise and quick decision-making were crucial in extinguishing the fire and preventing further spread. Meanwhile, as the smoke permeated into the guest areas of the ship, the guest services team provided comfort and reassurance that the situation was under control and that their safety was not at risk. Over the public announcement system, the captain informed everyone aboard that the situation was being handled and made a plea to everyone to remain calm and continue to enjoy the evening. This level of organisation and communication helped prevent panic and ensured that the evacuation of the areas affected by the smoke was conducted professionally and in an orderly fashion. After the unfortunate event, the engineering team worked tirelessly to assess and repair the damage.

This experience highlights the importance of preparedness and teamwork in handling emergencies; the training each crew member receives is invaluable, but it is also the trust and mutual support among the team members that truly makes the difference. Each member of the crew knows their role and trusts their colleague to perform theirs, thus creating a coordinated and effective response to whatever crisis may arise. In the aftermath of this event, a thorough review was conducted to identify areas for improvement. The senior officers assembled to analyse the incident and the debriefing then became an essential learning tool and a key element to ensure that all the crew was even better prepared for future emergencies. The teamwork displayed during the fire onboard not only safeguarded the lives of the guests and crew, but also strengthened our bonds and resilience as a team.

Learning and development

Developing teams is a continuous process of helping employees to improve their skills and build good relationships with one another. An important part of the development process is training them to adopt a growth mindset. According to Carol Dweck (2006), we can improve our skills and intelligence by working hard and being committed to growth. As business entrepreneurs, we must encourage this mindset within a team which increases resilience, creativity and strong collaboration among teammates. I was fortunate to be presented with opportunities for continuous learning and development through training programmes organised by the cruise line I worked for. Those open-minded organisations who enhance their employees' skills and knowledge by investing in their professional growth become better positioned for business success. For example, whether developed in-house or externalised, various courses focused on communication skills, conflict resolution and leadership are essential for equipping employees with the tools needed to navigate challenges effectively.

Another important part of development is creating a space in which team members feel comfortable sharing their thoughts and feelings. This allows them to talk about any worries, find ways to perform better and celebrate their achievements. Helpful feedback shows team members what they are good at and what they need to improve, which helps them grow both personally and professionally. Kolb (1984) highlights the fact that when team members think about their experiences with the intention to learn, it helps them improve and come up with new ideas.

Team-building activities are important for growth and can include activities like outdoor adventures and problem-solving games. These activities help improve relationships and build trust among team members. In a casual setting, employees step outside their usual work routine and engage with fellow colleagues on a personal level, developing a camaraderie between them, not as formal as in the office.

It is also essential to delegate important tasks, which can boost the confidence of aspiring managers and give them diverse roles and responsibilities. This can take various forms such as rotational leadership programmes, in which appointed team members alternate in directing projects or facilitating meetings.

I was offered many such opportunities, where I had to step up and perform at the level of management, and, by doing so consistently, business organisations equip future leaders with the skills necessary to guide their teams through challenges and empower them to become experts in their field. Team development is a multifaceted process that starts with a growth mindset and covers a broad range of approaches that target long-term success.

Talent retention

Retaining talent has become a top priority for organisations, especially in recent years with the workforce migration following the Covid-19 pandemic, and particularly because high turnover rates are costly and disruptive. One of the most effective ways to keep employees is to create a lively, positive and engaging work environment. It is well known that people are looking for organisations that provide opportunities for career growth and development, and they are more likely to stay where they feel valued, supported and motivated. Another approach is to offer competitive compensation and benefits that suit their needs and help sustain their livelihood.

I can relate to this, and I remember how motivated I felt when my performance was appreciated and even small achievements were recognised early in my career. It made work feel like a rewarding experience, and for me at the time, it was an important factor in keeping me working for the organisation. Acknowledgement can take many forms, and employee of the month awards, informal gestures of gratitude, customised thank-you cards or public commendations during team meetings are great ways to do this. According to Kouzes and Posner (2007), employees who believe that their efforts are acknowledged and rewarded are more engaged and dedicated to the businesses they work for. Nowadays, from the get-go, candidates are keen to know about their long-term prospects within a company, as well as their chances of professional advancement. Many leave after just under a year of working with a company that fails to motivate them. And who can blame them? Why would anyone choose to invest their time and effort in a company when there are no realistic opportunities for professional growth? Compared to three decades ago, the workforce mentality has changed substantially towards a more flexible approach that tolerates, or even encourages, remote working. Recent technological improvements have allowed a greater emphasis on work-life balance, and employees today choose autonomy and outcomes above working traditional office hours.

Work-life balance has become an important issue when discussing talent retention, and showing respect and concern for employees' personal time gives organisations a competitive edge. Flexible working hours, remote working possibilities and wellness programmes have all been found to help employees achieve this balance. Developing a healthy company culture is critical for talent retention, and employees who perceive that their well-being is a top priority are more satisfied and loyal to the organisation for longer. Encouraging open communication, teamwork and celebrating diversity are also key elements of a positive culture. Robinson, Perryman and Hayday (2004) argue that when employees feel that they are part of a supportive and inclusive community, they are more likely to stay with that organisation.

Talent retention is truly about creating a positive and engaging work environment, recognising and appreciating employees' contributions, providing opportunities for career growth, promoting work-life balance and fostering a positive organisational culture. Long-term business success is achieved by focusing on these areas and recognising the importance of building a loyal and committed workforce.

Empowering

I remember early in my career how happy and motivated I felt when I was entrusted with some task that was out of the ordinary. Employees like having the autonomy, resources and support they need to take charge of their job and make decisions. Among other things, empowerment implies giving people tasks and trusting them to make smart choices and be creative to get the best results. Spreitzer (1995) found that when workers feel strong and supported, they are more involved, motivated and manage to get more work done.

Employees feel more in control when they feel involved in making decisions and are asked for their opinion about important issues. It is no small thing when management delegate authority to make choices to an employee. We like it when our opinions are valued and when we are involved in the way things are done, and this is when we are more likely to be fully invested in our work. It is equally important to provide the necessary resources and support so the employee can complete the activity successfully.

Unlike our parents' generation, employees today are fortunate enough to enjoy easier access to the tools and information they need to be able to perform at their best. If implemented correctly, this important factor often translates into higher productivity and efficiency in remote-working contexts. Another important part of empowerment is breaking down formal boundaries and building a culture of trust and responsibility. From a leader's standpoint, allowing workers to make decisions and take responsibility for their work generates a feeling of ownership and pride, which is equally satisfying for the management and the employee. It is important not to neglect the delicate balance between trust and accountability, and holding employees accountable for their performance keeps them dedicated to maintaining standards.

Another important element of empowerment is the need to recognise and celebrate employees' accomplishments. When employees realise that their efforts and contributions are acknowledged and valued, they feel inspired to perform at their very best.

Autonomy

Related to empowerment is autonomy, and the latter is a direct effect of the former. Autonomy is the degree of freedom and independence employees have to make decisions and manage their work. It should not be difficult to find examples in your professional life when you have been given a task and have been entrusted to complete it. This involves a level of trust between management and the employee, allowing them to take ownership of tasks, use their judgement and make choices that meet both the employee's professional goals and the organisation's objectives. Deci and Ryan (2000) highlight that if workers have the freedom to make choices, they feel more motivated, involved in their tasks and satisfied with their jobs. This benefits them and the company, giving people responsibility, increasing productivity and bringing better results. When workers are allowed to make choices, they also take responsibility for the consequences of those choices. Feeling like they own something inspires people to work harder and try to do better. Teammates are then motivated to go above and beyond when they feel that they have control over their work and that their contributions matter.

Workers who can do their jobs without constant supervision come up with more creative ideas and try new things. This often creates great new answers to existing problems, and being able to think creatively leads to important improvements in processes, as well as in the products we make and the services we provide.

Amabile (1996) found that companies who encourage people to work on their own are more creative and generate new ideas. This helps the organisations stand out from their competitors. Management should be setting clear goals and providing employees with the tools they need to work independently, offering them help and guidance whenever they need it. It doesn't mean that they are left alone to decide whatever they want, whenever they choose, and be given absolute independence. Finding the right balance between letting workers make their own choices and providing them with the guidance and tools they need is essential. One way this can be done is having regular meetings, giving feedback and keeping communication clear. A real-life example of autonomy can be found in the tech industry, where Google and Atlassian implemented '20% time' policies, allowing employees to spend a portion of their workweek on projects of their choice, even if those projects are not directly related to their primary job responsibilities. This approach, according to Mediratta (2007), resulted in the development of innovative products and features, such as Gmail and Google News.

Well-being and work satisfaction are directly linked to autonomy. Let's think about it: if you were given the freedom to choose how to approach your job, would you not choose to personalise your work to match your abilities and interests, resulting in a more fun and satisfying workplace? This sense of autonomy gives employees satisfaction, and reduces stress and burnout by allowing them to take control of their responsibilities and successfully manage their time. However, it is fair to say that not every employee will immediately feel comfortable with a high level of autonomy, and that many employees enjoy being supervised often. Depending on their upbringing, level of confidence, personal strengths and limitations, there might be certain people who may require a more personalised approach, more guidance and help as they gain the confidence and capabilities needed to work more independently. In these circumstances, management should gradually increase the level of autonomy given to the employee, offering adequate training and resources. These employees need to feel encouraged to take some risks and be allowed to learn from their mistakes without fearing that they will be held responsible or that they will be reprimanded. In general, giving employees some freedom is a strong motivator for them. It is important to find the right mix of independence and support so that workers feel confident while also having the help they need to succeed, and when used right, greater autonomy helps create a more lively, creative and happy workplace for everyone.

Summary

This chapter has looked at the dynamic world of teams, including the issues they confront and the tactics that might help them grow. It discussed the value of successful leadership, the balance between power and empathy, and the vital role of company culture. The importance of multiculturality and collaboration in an emergency was highlighted in the case study, in which we looked at a fire on board a cruise ship. We then talked about the ongoing process of team development, highlighting the value of a growth mindset, continual learning and feedback. Talent retention was also in the spotlight, with an emphasis on fostering a healthy work environment, acknowledging individuals' achievements and giving chances for advancement. The concept of empowerment was then explored, underlining the importance of autonomy, resources, support, trust and accountability.

It's important for business organisations to understand these principles if they are looking to build strong teams that focus on new ideas and creativity, and to maintain high levels of production and service over time. Strong and independent teams are vital for every organisation. When companies invest in their growth and happiness, they create a lively and cooperative workplace that attracts both employees and customers alike.

4
The Individual

Welcome to Chapter 4, where the complexities of human nature are examined in depth. Let us move our attention away from organisations and team dynamics and zoom in on the individual – the fundamental unit of our society. Individuals need attention because they contain the essential essence of mankind. We will explore what makes each person special and how they can grow, which is inspiring, and we'll talk about my favourite topic: the power of one. We've all learned from history amazing examples of courage, and of sacrifices made by simple people who influenced for the better the lives of many.

The power of one: You CAN make a difference

Individual power is critical to how our communities and business organisations grow and function. Whether we are aware of it or not, each individual unknowingly adds to the bigger picture, influencing outcomes and relationships well beyond the contacts we experience on a regular basis. Thinking about it, it can be noticed in everyday acts and decisions that cumulatively have a major influence. This power may or may not be manifested in an eventful manner, but sometimes we hear stories about how one person managed to actually make a difference, and, just as this has been true throughout history, so it is in today's times of transformation. Personal power is often referred to as the capacity to inspire people, question the norms and leave a lasting impression. The goal is to recognise our own capabilities and use them to better our personal and professional lives in such a way as to fulfil our purpose in society and emanate goodness and positive energy around.

Have you ever thought about how a single person could start a movement? Consider Rosa Parks' solitary act of resistance, refusing to give up her bus seat, which sparked the Montgomery bus boycott and served as a starting point in the Civil Rights Movement (Parks & Haskins, 1992). This highlights how a single person's courage and determination is able to change the world and inspire others to act. Or the impact of young Greta

Thunberg, who began as a teenager to advocate for action against the dramatic effects of climate change, and through her actions gained international attention. She was just a young child when she started, and because of her courage and determination, millions of people around the world have become more aware and have been taking part in the battle against climate change.

Also, Dr Martin Luther King Jr, whose courage and strong ideals in fairness and justice inspired many people and played a significant role in the American Civil Rights Movement. Or Marie Curie, whose groundbreaking radioactivity research awarded her two Nobel Prizes and paved the way for advances in health and science; her work has saved countless lives and continues to impact scientific study today. These historical personalities demonstrate how one person's passion, vision, sacrifice and perseverance can lead to monumental changes.

This power of one is not encouraged in traditional schools. After all, why would it be? It can be disturbing for the establishment when people realise just how powerful they really are. People can express their power in the workplace by using their unique skills and perspectives to contribute to their team's success. For example, an employee who brings a fresh perspective or an innovative approach to a problem and helps to solve it can inspire the colleagues to think differently and adopt new methods. This type of influence is important to cultivate a culture of constant growth and development in any business enterprise. Recognising your particular strengths, as well as opportunities for progress, is essential for understanding your personal power. You have to be intentional about it and activate your self-awareness, and you can do this through introspection to identify your strengths while seeking opportunities to grow and improve. You could easily use tools such as the SWOT analysis (Strengths, Weaknesses, Opportunities and Threats) to help you and the organisations you work for to better assess your capabilities and identify areas for personal and professional development (Humphrey, 2005).

The individual's influence extends, of course, to the personal life as well, and making conscious decisions that correspond with our beliefs and aspirations allows us to live more satisfying and meaningful lives. The sensation of living a purpose-driven life provides a genuine sense of empowerment, which improves our well-being and contentment, causing a positive vibe that inspires others around us. Think about how one person's kind actions can help a community; little, surprising acts of kindness, like buying coffee for a stranger, or regularly shopping for groceries for an elderly neighbour, or helping out at a nearby homeless shelter, or just simply teaching a child something you know well, can truly inspire others to be kind too. When people see kind acts, they usually want to be kind as well, making everyone in the community feel happier.

The power of one, whether positive or negative, is visible in our daily lives. Every day in our local communities we may encounter people who are not so nice and who project the worst version of themselves into the world, and there are certainly others who stand out from the crowd shining their light of goodness and positivity to those around through their well-intended efforts. This world needs love, we all need love, and we all have the power to make the world what we envision it to be. It might be a neighbour who organises community activities, or a teacher who goes above and beyond to inspire their pupils, or a small company owner who donates to local organisations, or even you and me doing our bit. There is poverty, hunger and suffering in the world, and if we look carefully we might just discover some unfortunate people in need of help closer than we might think.

The point is this: you too have the power to make a real difference. This is critical to remember – every one of us has the power to light up the darkness. Invest yourself in others and you will get the feeling of achievement you have been looking for. You don't have to be famous or in a position of high power to effect change; start with modest steps, like listening to someone who needs to talk (other than your close friends), stand up for what you believe in, or devote some of your time to a person in need or a cause you care about. Every little thing you do counts – what you may think is insignificant, may mean the world to the other person, at a moment where they need it the most. Your actions can inspire others to bring about positive change and enhance the lives of those around you.

It is important to observe how people think and interact with others in their environment, and to notice how different factors in a person's upbringing influence their behaviour and decisions. Malala Yousafzai's story (2013) says a lot about her: despite many obstacles, she pushed hard for her right to attend school and inspired millions across the world to help females get access to education. Her personal example led to global movements and important changes in education systems in various countries, and it shows how one person's courage can truly make a big difference and question the way things are usually done. It is critical that we recognise and act to solve the challenges that arise in our everyday lives and collaborate with each other to improve everyone's well-being and quality of life. We just have to make a genuine effort to understand the influence of social, cultural and economic variables on human behaviour and life itself, and we may surprise ourselves with our compulsion to help in some way. This human trait, this need to help others, is instilled in each of us, and what counts the most is our freedom of choice, which ultimately determines the outcome of our endeavours. Paradoxically, the world today is in a bad shape. We are at a crossroads, more divided than ever and being eroded by various crises. We all have been given the ability to make a difference in our and others' lives, and in so doing, one by one, we can have a beneficial influence that spreads across the world.

In a business setting, valuing each person's work and their soft skills makes people more motivated. When they feel that their skills and opinions matter, they feel empowered to perform better and stay loyal to their employer, willing to go the extra mile and perform their best.

Each individual's role in creating change and success is essential, and it can only be achieved by embracing our unique potential and making choices with genuinely good intentions. That is when we create positive ripple effects that stretch well beyond our immediate surroundings. The power of one is more than a concept: it's a reality that we can all embrace and live by. It can be a tremendous force in our communities and society at large. From offering compassion and support, to launching movements and inspiring change, one person's actions may have profound effects. Let us celebrate ourselves and acknowledge that we all have the potential to make a difference. Collectively, we can make the world a better place, one act of kindness at a time.

Change catalyst

As we have seen, the power of the individual is linked to our capacity to influence and inspire change through our actions and decisions. Essentially, the majority of us want to live in a better world, but it all gets a bit blurry when it is time to act and actually *do* something.

Somehow we undermine our power and fail to believe that it all really starts with us, and with an understanding that we can use our ability to influence the social context in which we live, to evolve and contribute to a culture of creativity and resilience. Working with ourselves is critical, in the sense that, in these days of rapid transformation, it is important to silence our fears and move forward knowing that things will somehow fall into place. Throughout history, our ancestors have lived through tremendous changes, their safety was often threatened and poverty was, for most, the norm. Yet somehow they managed to live through it, leaving us a more abundant and thriving world. Change is unavoidable. We need to accept the factual reality and adjust to new situations with a good attitude. We need to find the best way to cope with whatever life throws at us. The Covid-19 pandemic, although it had dramatic effects, taught us the need to have a different attitude towards change, and how important it is to be open to new ideas, taking chances and remaining resilient in the face of adversity.

Adopting a change mentality is a challenging process, especially when our human nature prefers stability and predictability. However, it is no longer a matter of choice, but has become an imperative that reverberates throughout our personal and professional lives. Change brings along opportunities for new experiences and connections that can enrich our lives and careers. For example, changing career or taking on a new role within the same organisation helps reignite that inner drive, providing a fresh start to use the skills you have to enhance your professional development. A change mentality is extremely important in our lives and it is connected with a growth mindset.

This mentality rests on the love of learning and accepting difficulties by persevering in the face of failures (Dweck, 2006), which ultimately improves confidence and resilience. Being receptive to feedback and accepting new challenges may lead us to take on new learning challenges, start a new course, attend seminars or specialised counselling sessions, which will help us in the long run to increase our knowledge and abilities and make it easier to adjust to change. Sometimes, you need to be flexible, this could very well mean that you might have to let go of old habits or practices that no longer serve you, and readjust your plans and revisit your life goals. The ability to reroute your course in response to ever-changing circumstances is a valuable trait, one that younger generations are more inclined to welcome into their lives and work with on a daily basis. This process gets easier with a support system, and it is therefore important to surround yourself with positive influences – your family, a coach or mentor, or some of your close friends who encourage you along the way – that will make things more manageable and easier for you to transition through change.

Think of a catalyst as something or someone that provokes or speeds significant change. In the workplace, people can act as catalysts by displaying their unique perspectives and skills and advancing groundbreaking ideas that could lead to significant improvements. Creating a positive work environment is essential for channelling this kind of catalytic energy. Whenever I feel encouraged to share my ideas and take risks, I am more likely to come up with innovative solutions and I make sure I replicate this in my professional life and with my son. Elon Musk's vision and innovative thinking have transformed whole industries, from electric vehicles to space exploration, and along with technical abilities, much of it can be attributed to his ability to challenge the status quo and pursue ambitious goals, making him a change catalyst in multiple fields (Vance, 2015).

That is why management positions should not minimise the importance of empowering employees to act with courage and provide them with the resources and authority they need to take ownership of their initiatives to affect change in the workplace. This autonomy is critical because it instils a sense of duty and accountability in employees, driving them to succeed.

CASE STUDY: Clarity

Being an inspirational coach is a rewarding experience. I was once working with a client who was facing career stagnation, which happens more often than people like to admit. Working in a large corporation, he reached a point where his work no longer felt fulfilling and he was constantly lacking motivation. He felt that his life had lost its direction, and he confided that he was becoming depressed as a result. He was trapped in his role, unable to see a path forward, and in our counselling sessions we used some tools that encouraged self-reflection and that tested his values. Together, we identified his core beliefs, strengths and long-term aspirations, making use of the Wheel of Life and value-based goal setting. He was able to find those areas of imbalance and rekindle some long-forgotten passions. We worked together to develop a clear vision for his future, setting some achievable short-term goals that were aligned with his values. Over time, he felt encouraged to engage in new experiences outside of work to reignite his passion and creativity. He also volunteered some of his time in a field he was passionate about, and even picked up a hobby. Within a few months, he had a renewed sense of purpose and felt energised. At work, he proposed some new ideas and took some proactive steps to reshape his role within the team. The following year, he was promoted to a more challenging role and his performance at work improved dramatically. In the end, he was proud for gaining the courage to take the bull by the horns and realise that he had the power all along to change some things in his life.

So, whenever you feel like you are stagnating and lacking motivation, remember that you owe it to yourself to fight it off and remain flexible. Try your best to embrace change, putting all your energy and focus into searching for a new perspective and, step by step, turn it into an opportunity for personal and professional growth. When we exert our personal power, we act as change agents, able to transform our environments at work and at home for our benefit and the benefit of people around us.

Resilience

Throughout our lives, our individual and collective endurance is put to the test in ways we never believed possible, with all kinds of crises we have had to overcome. Nonetheless, each time we emerge stronger and more resilient than before, even when some of us sadly pay the price of losing someone dear. As difficult as it is, we cannot give up on ourselves and those we love, and we need to continue to fight the fight of faith, believing that all will be OK in the end. We have to find the inner strength and activate our ability to recover from hardship, adapt to change and persist in the face of adversity. After all, this is what builds our resilience, and preserving our sense of well-being is an essential attribute that keeps us striving ahead.

Building resilience is definitely not an easy undertaking, and it cannot be acquired overnight. It only develops by facing challenges and adopting a positive mindset while doing so, and building strong relationships and enhancing problem-solving skills is a major part of this process. A positive mindset helps us view challenges not as obstacles, but as opportunities to grow, and this perspective can make a significant difference in how we approach and overcome difficulties (Dweck, 2006).

It is important to know that we are not alone, and we should try to make meaningful connections that are essential for our emotional well-being. Relationships are crucial in providing the support networks that we can rely on during tough times. Whether it's colleagues, friends or family members, having people who offer encouragement and advice helps us stay resilient.

Author Kitty Kelley (2011) outlines how Oprah's resilience and determination inspired millions to persevere through their own difficulties and strive for success. Oprah is a perfect example of resilience; a person who chose not to give up and addressed the challenges she faced head on, with courage and proactivity, and managed to overcome significant personal and professional challenges to become one of the most influential figures in media.

Being a leader also means being a mentor, supporting employees to build resilience through valuable resources like training programmes, wellness initiatives and development opportunities. We live in the knowledge economy, and we must be smart if we are to take advantage of the large variety of resources available to us and develop the skills and mindset we need to navigate all the adversities life throws our way.

CASE STUDY: Mindfulness and balance

Looking back, I'd like to share with you a personal story that shows the transformative power we all have inbuilt, deep within our human fabric. Years back, I was feeling overwhelmed by my intensive lifestyle; between the demands of my job, my personal life and the classes at the university I was attending, it was difficult to balance it all. Every day was a constant juggling of responsibilities, and everything was competing for first place, making me feel stressed and drained, impacting my overall state of well-being. In search of finding a suitable solution to help re-establish the balance in my life and bring back the passion and relentlessness, I decided to explore mindfulness practices coupled with prayer. Mindfulness is the practice of being present and fully engaged in the current moment and it has been shown to reduce stress, improve focus and enhance emotional regulation (Kabat-Zinn, 1994). I started with simple mindfulness exercises involving deep breathing and short meditation sessions, and concluding with a brief conscious prayer, and I gradually incorporated these practices into my daily routine.

The effects were significant, and as I became more connected with the divine, I began to notice a reduction in my stress levels. It became easier to manage my workload and I approached challenges with a clearer perspective and a calmer mindset. My productivity improved as well and I was better focused, and this allowed me to enjoy my work more. I also noticed how my relationships with colleagues and loved ones improved because I was more present and attentive in my interactions.

One day, during a high-stakes project at work, some unexpected issues came up threatening our timeline. In the midst of everything that was going on, thanks to mindfulness practice and prayer, I was able to remain hopeful, calm and focused. I gathered the team, sat around in a circle encouraging open communication between us all, and collaboratively we developed a plan to address the issues. Not only did we complete the project on time, but this trial also strengthened our team's cohesion and bond.

This personal transformation through mindfulness has been a game-changer for me in the sense that it has equipped me with the tools to manage stress factors, stay focused and maintain emotional balance. To this day, I continue to practise mindfulness and prayer regularly, and it remains a keystone of my personal and professional well-being. I strongly recommend this powerful practise to anyone who wants to bring personal transformation into their daily life, reduce stress, and improve focus. Among many other benefits, mindfulness coupled with prayer truly helps me to navigate my busy lifestyle and achieve resilience and fulfilment in my personal and professional life.

Real life applicability of traditional education systems

Just like me, you have probably experienced the lack of practical knowledge in various key areas, like management, finance and the personal development of soft skills. The fact is that the traditional education system is not optimised to prepare children for these areas of adult life. Education has a crucial role in one's life, but there is a growing acknowledgement that traditional schooling systems frequently fail to teach critical life skills such as economic literacy, emotional intelligence, practical problem-solving and so on. This education gap leaves many young people unprepared to deal with real life and workplace demands. One of the primary challenges is that the education system places a high value on rote learning and standardised testing, in which students are taught to memorise facts and pass examinations, but are rarely taught how to use this knowledge in real-world situations. In my experience – and you may well relate to it too – this focus on academic accomplishment ignores the development of critical thinking and practical skills, both of which are necessary for success in life (Robinson, 2011).

Let's us take financial education, for example, which is an important skill that is seldom taught in traditional schools. Many young people join a profession without having a basic concept of budgeting, saving, investing or debt management, and, later in life, this lack of knowledge causes poor financial decisions and long-term financial insecurity. Taking things further, there is a connection between poverty and poor financial choices, stemming from a lack of basic economic knowledge. In order to fill this gap, which has long-term societal effects, it is imperative that we integrate financial education, critical thinking and soft skills into school curricula. This will provide students with the knowledge they need to make more educated financial decisions and attain economic stability.

Emotional intelligence is another important factor that is sometimes missed in traditional schooling. It is particularly important for students to detect, identify and control their own emotions, as well as having the ability to empathise with others and understand various social situations. According to author Daniel Goleman (1995), these skills are essential for developing strong relationships and managing stress, and there are numerous extracurricular programmes that teach emotional intelligence to help students develop greater self-awareness and interpersonal skills.

CASE STUDY: Team cohesion

In addition to one-on-one coaching, I sometimes facilitate group counselling sessions. One of the group sessions was aimed at improving the team dynamics within a start-up organisation. The business was experiencing growing pains, and the team, made up of different individuals with strong personalities, was dealing with communication challenges and opposing work styles, resulting in frequent friction and a loss in productivity. Most of the time, there were significant challenges in collaboration and communication, causing delays in projects and creating a tense work environment. The group sessions focused mainly on communication, to build trust and mutual respect, with practical exercises aimed at improving knowledge of various working styles and developing collaborating methods. It turned out that all they needed was to share their problems and expectations without feeling singled out. The Myers-Briggs Type Indicator (MBTI) helped them better understand their own personalities, as well as those of their colleagues, and after a while, jokes and laughter were part of the sessions.

To be able to overcome real-life issues, one must also possess some practical problem-solving abilities, and although traditional education serves as a foundation, it is the capacity to apply this knowledge to solve problems that really prepares people for success. The education system might assist children in developing these skills through project-based learning, which confronts real-world situations and encourages them to generate solutions based on research, teamwork and critical thinking, but to bridge the gap between school and real life, a more comprehensive approach to learning is required, and significant progress may be made by adding experiential learning and real-world activities that relate classroom learning to adult life.

Healthy thinking

We live in a knowledge economy, and every day we are assaulted with information from all sides – social media, television, commercials and so on. If we allow it, this never-ending stream can easily take over our ability to focus, shaping the way we think, feel and make decisions. It is difficult to know what to believe, and misinformation and 'fake news' travel around the world in a matter of minutes, making critical thinking skills essential. Everything competes for our attention, time and money, and it is important to verify the source of any information before we form an opinion, and also consider other opposing views. The world of marketing has become so refined that subtle marketing techniques are designed to draw us into endless scrolling through social media feeds, often without us even realising. Competing organisations race to craft their ads to keep us clicking, liking and sharing, in a targeted effort to capture our data and make money, which makes it easy for us to get distracted and overwhelmed. We should be vigilant, filter everything through our values system, take regular prolonged screen breaks whenever possible, and practise mindfulness to stay focused and clear-headed. Recognising these subtle marketing techniques and noticing the constant competition for our attention is the first step toward taking back control.

Our minds are powerful tools, and it's up to us to protect them by thinking healthy, questioning what we read and taking time to unplug and navigate this information-rich world more effectively. Healthy thinking is essential for a balanced and fulfilling life, and in order to enhance our mental and physical health, build strong relationships and achieve our goals, we must pay attention to what we feed our mind, to cultivate a positive mindset, to manage stress effectively, etc. At first, this will not be an easy undertaking, but by implementing small steps with determination, healthy habits will develop. In today's crazy busy world, cultivating a positive outlook in life is more important than ever; sound and clear thinking helps us go through challenges with resilience.

That is why it is important to keep your mind focused and organised and always revisit your set of values and what you truly cherish the most. Brace yourself and stay strong in the face of adversity, never forget to maintain your healthy thinking and avoid feeling overwhelmed by noise and social pressure. Mental health has become an increasingly important topic in recent years, as many people around the world are dealing with depression and suicidal thought patterns, responsible for many broken destinies and lost lives. To boost our resilience and enhance our overall well-being, we should anchor our thinking in the positive things in our lives, acknowledge that we are fortunate to have our dear ones around us, and remember that we are not alone. And for those of us who *do* feel alone, know that you never are, and that God, or the higher power you may believe in, is always with you, stitched into every fibre of your being.

This perspective is known to improve mental health, and one effective way to cultivate a positive mindset is by practising gratitude and regularly writing down things you are grateful for. According to Emmons and McCullough (2003), this exercise helps shift attention away from negative ideas and toward pleasant experiences, generating a sense of gratitude and satisfaction. Even if it may not always seem so, everyone has their own set of challenges, so let us be smart about it and try our best to maintain a grateful attitude, appreciate our blessings and strive to focus on the positives of life, on the glass that is half full. Frequent stress has a negative impact on both mental and physical health, causing symptoms such as anxiety, sadness, depression and blood-pressure related illnesses, cardiovascular difficulties, etc. Research has shown that mindfulness meditation, deep breathing exercises, and regular physical activity reduces stress and enhances relaxation (Kabat-Zinn, 1990). Trying to relax and learning to develop good stress-management skills will benefit our well-being and quality of life in the long run.

It is no secret that understanding and managing our emotions, building strong relationships and seeking support when needed is vital for our emotional well-being, which is part of healthy thinking. Developing emotional intelligence early in childhood, or even in one's teens, enhances a general state of well-being later on in life, improving self-awareness and increasing our empathy towards others, helping us to fine-tune our communication skills.

I like to engage in activities that bring me joy and fulfilment: travelling the world, reading, writing, cooking, painting or listening to music are hobbies which help me maintain balance in my life. What keeps you smiling? Socialising and volunteering are also known to improve emotional well-being and it contributes to a more fulfilled life. Healthy thinking is also about setting realistic goals and having a sense of purpose instead of wandering aimlessly through life is crucial. It is worth mentioning that the goals you set should be aligned with your values and aspirations and should be reviewed regularly and adjusted as needed to ensure that they remain relevant and attainable. This book's goal, for example, is to analyse the customer experience from an organisational perspective, zoom in on the role of effective teams, reach deep into the core of the individual and highlight the transformative power of one, and shine a light on those key elements that inspire and empower people to become the very best version of themselves.

Summary

In this chapter, the spotlight has been on the individual and how products and services are designed with the customer's welfare in mind, to achieve exceptional levels of experience. We studied the individual's significance within organisational and team settings, as well as in broader society, and we looked at the power of individuals to influence others in the experience economy. The value of a supportive and empowered work environment was emphasised, investigating the individual's function as a generator of creativity and productivity. We then discussed resilience, highlighting the necessity of having a good mentality, strong connections and excellent problem-solving abilities to overcome obstacles.

5
The Power Of Example

Welcome to Chapter 5, in which we will explore the limitless power we each have to transform our lives and encourage others to regain control of their outcomes and do the same. Anyone can help make their community better – it's incredible to realise that one person's actions can affect a lot of other people, and a person's impact and importance in today's experience-driven world is significant. Our own thoughts, creativity and actions serve to influence both our personal lives and the world around us. Let us look into how we can all use our strengths to find our own path and play a positive role in our communities.

Reconnecting

Today, it is all too easy to become disconnected from our humanity, from the people around us, from the natural world and from the higher power that created us. This disconnection often feels like isolation, anxiety and a lack of fulfilment in our lives, and it is important to take time to reconnect with ourselves. It counts more than we can imagine if we keep close to the people we love, if we remain in synergy with nature and the divine, and strive to maintain a sense of balance and fulfilment in our lives. Staying true to ourselves and taking intentional steps to keep or rebuild these connections helps us gain that sense of belonging, purpose and well-being. It is a difficult but satisfying process that has enormous effects for our lives, and it all begins with the power of intention. There is unimaginable beauty in simplicity. These true connections determine who we are as people, bringing us closer to living a truly meaningful life, whether we are reconnecting with nature, fostering relationships or seeking inner peace.

Reconnecting with nature helps our health and well-being, and science has shown us that spending time in nature improves our mood, decreases our stress levels and improves our immune systems and overall strength. Activities like hiking or gardening, or simply going for a walk in the park, help us feel more grounded and connected to nature. Author Richard Louv's book *Last Child in the Woods* (2008) highlights the need to protect our children from nature-deficit disease, as nature offers a feeling of calm and perspective, reminding us of the beauty of creation and the interdependence of life.

Spending time with friends and family members, getting that sense of belonging and support, helps us see life's challenges in a different light, which is crucial for our emotional well-being and resilience. This intentional living is filled with priceless memories with the ones we love, and the crazy lifestyles we have today exert a big strain on our relationships in such a way that spending quality time together is being put to the test every day. A friend in need is a friend indeed, but few people make time for others these days. Spiritual reconnection often begins with the turmoil we feel in our lives, some trouble that forces us into an intentional introspection and talk with God. Whatever belief system you follow, taking the time to reflect on your thoughts and behaviours and connect with a higher power allows you to better understand yourself, recognise your genuine aspirations and align them with your life's purpose.

Psalm 46:10 tells us to 'Be still, and know that I am God', emphasising the necessity of quietening our minds and emotions in order to hear the divine guidance inside. Reconnecting with the divine through prayer and meditation helps us express our innermost feelings and seek help on our journey, especially in troubling times. As Philippians 4:6–7 advises, 'Do not be anxious about anything, but in every situation, by prayer and petition, with thanksgiving present your requests to God. And the peace of God, which transcends all understanding, will guard your hearts and your minds in Christ Jesus.' If we try to recognise the divine presence in all aspects of life, we can find purpose and meaning in everything and everyone. Colossians 3:17 reminds us of the following: 'And whatever you do, whether in word or deed, do it all in the name of the Lord Jesus, giving thanks to God the Father through Him'.

A holistic approach to well-being encourages both our own progress and our contributions to the world around us, in the sense that, if we wish our lives to have spiritual purpose and guidance, we must first call on God and seek a profound spiritual connection before matching our efforts with divine guidance and grace. We are wonderfully designed humans, and we will gain a sense of inner serenity and fulfilment that spreads outward if we align with God's purpose for our lives. If we prioritise our spiritual relationship with God, it ties us to a higher purpose that transcends material concerns and it generates a beneficial ripple that spreads throughout our communities.

Oh, how wonderful it is to have that feeling of balance and inner calm in life! Start today with your prayers and mindfulness meditations, and you may want to journal your thoughts and feelings to help you reconnect with your inner self and maintain emotional equilibrium.

CASE STUDY: Finding strength in God

A personal experience can perhaps better illustrate the profound impact of this process, which helped me develop a deeper understanding of myself and my place in the world. A few years ago, life's journey took me through a painful and dramatic separation experience and I couldn't help but feel overwhelmed by the demands of maintaining a balance between work, academic studies and raising my son as a single parent, and all this caused a constant state of stress and disconnection. After reaching a burnout stage, I took a step back to reset my goals and reshuffle my priorities. I slowed down and took the time to connect with my deepest aspirations, the wants and needs that had gotten lost somewhere along the way, and I identified what mattered the most to me.

Recharging in a natural setting and spending some time outdoors provided a sense of calm and joy, helping me feel alive and in synergy with the universe. I did not have to search a lot, as God – our healer and our provider – is always within a thought's reach, and He never fails us or underdelivers on His promises. In Hebrews 13:5, God said: 'Never will I leave you; never will I forsake you'. And that, my dear friend, is everything you need to know when hitting rock bottom: you are never alone.

Before I knew it, my depression, fear and anxiety had dissipated back to where it had come from. Zig Ziglar's (1997) famous fear quote states that F-E-A-R has two meanings: 'Forget Everything And Run or Face Everything And Rise'. The choice is ours to make. There are times in everyone's lives when we need to come out from the fear zone into the faith zone, and write our life story about how adversity propelled us into our destiny.

So, feeling hopeful and renewed, I went on to make some important conscious decisions to rebuild my life stronger than before. I reconnected with friends and family, prioritising quality time together and engaging in meaningful conversations, and these interactions gave me strength and provided an enormous sense of support.

Through this process, I regained control of my life, and once I felt set on the right course, that is when the idea of the C.A.R.E. Model began forming in my mind.

Growth/success mindset

Growing our wings in life is a vital, three-dimensional part of human development that incorporates personal, professional and emotional development. Throughout life, it is critical to seek out chances to grow and acquire new skills. It is not always an easy task, and it involves deliberate choices and courage to move outside of your comfort zone, strengthening your talents and broadening your limits in order to fly high and achieve what you were created for.

CASE STUDY: Emotional healing

One of my clients was undergoing a significant crisis caused by the end of a long-term relationship, and was feeling lost, overwhelmed and uncertain about the future. Although some time had passed, the emotional toll of the breakup was affecting all areas of her life, from her job performance to her social interactions.

She was struggling with feelings of grief, self-doubt and fear of the unknown, and the emotional distress was bursting out in anxiety, stopping her from moving forward.

She felt stuck in a negative cycle, and so together we looked for optimal solutions to guide her through a process of emotional healing focused on building acceptance, resilience and self-compassion. Prayer and mindfulness approaches helped reduce anxiety and stress, as did cognitive behavioural measures to confront and reframe her negative thought patterns. She began to reconnect with her social support network and participate in activities that encouraged self-acceptance. She gradually improved her emotional well-being and began to embrace new prospects for personal and professional development that before seemed impossible to her. A few months later, she felt a lot more confident and had a higher sense of self-worth and optimism about the future.

In life, there are some moments of crisis when we are forced to grow, although things may not appear clear at the time and it may seem like there are no solutions in sight. That's when we are called to dig deep into our talents, reactivate our dusty dreams and concentrate our focus inwards. Developing self-awareness, building new skills and pursuing our buried interests and passions will help us regain control. I can relate to this situation all too well, when life had thrown one of its best punches at me, and I found myself dusting off the shattered remnants of my hopes and dreams.

At that time, I remembered what God said: 'My grace is sufficient for you, for my power is made perfect in weakness' (2 Corinthians 12:9). That was when I restarted building my life and strengthening myself with this verse: 'He brought me up also out of a horrible pit, out of the miry clay, and set my feet upon a rock, and established my goings' (Psalms 40:2).

If you are going through some tough times, and you most definitely will at some point, as no one is exempt from suffering during their lifetime, remember: there is hope and you are not alone. Seek help and dig deep into yourself to find your pure human essence, because that is where you will find your utmost strength. Once you reconnect with yourself, you can start building your better self. Personal growth is not limited to acquiring knowledge; it also means allowing yourself to explore and engage in new experiences. For instance, author Stephen Covey (1989) highlights that it helps greatly to be proactive and 'begin with the end in mind', in other words 'keep your eyes on the prize' and be committed to achieving your goals. Try as much as you can to travel to new places, engage in new activities and meet new people, and rest assured you will broaden your perspective and long-term personal development.

Networking with colleagues and mentors is invaluable for providing you with insights and opportunities for career development. Just as much as personal growth is important, professional growth is essential for our career advancement and job satisfaction. It can be pursued through formal education and training programmes, without excluding the practical aspect of it: the priceless on-the-job experiences. This is an ongoing process, which develops if we continuously improve our skills, stay up to date with industry trends and seek new challenges and opportunities. We may not realise it, but by socialising, whether at work or in our private time, we are building emotional intelligence (EQ), which is important for our overall emotional growth. Understanding and managing our emotions, building strong relationships and coping with life's challenges helps us develop emotional resilience and avoid feeling crushed whenever challenges rise up in front of us. Surely, we can successfully employ practices such as mindfulness, journaling and therapy for our emotional comfort, but a strong network of friends, family and mentors, as author Daniel Goleman (1995) highlights, can provide an enormous source of support and encouragement.

A key aspect of growth is having a healthy perspective on what it means to adopt a success mindset, which is the belief that our abilities and intelligence can be developed through sustained effort and learning. Knowing this, we are more inclined to act, embrace challenges, persist in the face of setbacks and view failure as an opportunity for learning and improvement. Psychologist Carol Dweck (2006) emphasises that this mindset builds our resilience, motivates us, and brings us success in both our personal and professional endeavours.

A good example of growth can be seen in the story of JK Rowling, the author of the Harry Potter series, who, despite facing personal struggles and numerous rejections from publishers, persisted in her writing and ultimately achieved tremendous success. Her journey clearly illustrates the importance of resilience, perseverance, relentlessness, trusting one's abilities and maintaining a growth mindset in achieving personal goals and dreams (Rowling, 2015). Regardless of how daunting the challenge, we must be strong and have confidence in the continuous process of learning and self-discovery, seeking new opportunities and experiences to live a richer and more meaningful life.

The power of intentional choices

We are amazing, spiritual beings, created in the image of God and the sky is the limit to what we can achieve in our lifetimes if we believe in the beauty of our dreams and relentlessly work towards our goals. And in so doing, we may shine our light and encourage people around us to believe in themselves and in the divine, inspiring them to race ahead and follow their own ambitions. The power of deliberate decision steers us towards development and fulfilment. In order to live a more useful and happy life, we need to make intentional choices about what actually matters to us, and we need to connect our behaviours with our beliefs and aspirations.

In a world full of distractions and conflicting demands, whether we recognise it or not, we make important decisions every day, some of which are conscious, others automatic. Even doing nothing is a decision, but inactivity has long-term effects. We must recognise that if we do not use the power of intentional choice in alignment with our values, it may significantly distract us from our direction in life, leading us far away from what we have been created for. Each intentional choice should be taken to shape our journey in the direction that our gifts and abilities pull us, allowing us to live authentically, remembering that we are uniquely created. Being intentional in our choices and aligning our values, goals and aspirations with our actions helps us create a life that reflects our true selves and achieves our desired dreams. However, without a strong values system that is based on self-reflection and a clear sense of what matters the most, intentional choices may lead us astray or cause inner conflict. It is crucial to regularly reassess our values and goals to ensure that the intentional choices we make continue to align with our true purpose in life.

It is, however, quite possible to lack a clear dream to pursue in life, and that is perfectly alright. This just means that you must continue your life journey, allowing yourself to have new experiences and constantly learn until you stumble on that life-deciding moment when you figure out what would give you that purposeful sense of fulfilment. The key is to be perceptive, to understand your preferences and to listen to that inner voice that whispers your values, passions and dreams. And once you identify these core elements, you can make choices that are consistent with your authentic self and avoid being swayed by external pressures or instantly gratifying temptations.

A practical approach to intentional choice is setting clear and specific goals, which can act as a roadmap for you, guiding your decisions and actions towards your desired outcomes. In other words, establish the *what*, ask yourself *why*, and then focus on the *how*. For instance, if financial independence is your goal, intentional choices you might consider could include saving and investing wisely. Setting goals helps us prioritise actions and allocate resources effectively, ensuring that our efforts are focused on what truly matters (Locke & Latham, 2002). The conclusion one might come to, is that being mindful of how we spend our time and energy is an essential trait if we are to live in alignment with our core being, otherwise the distractions of life will sweep away our life's purpose. What I am referring to is that spending excessive time on social media or engaging in activities that do not contribute to personal growth may distract us from more meaningful pursuits.

Intentional choice also extends to relationships and social interactions, and surrounding ourselves with positive, supportive and like-minded individuals will significantly impact our well-being and success. We should try to gather around us people who share similar passions to our own, and we should choose relationships that nurture growth, creating a strong support network.

CASE STUDY: Crossroads

Here is a short personal story to illustrate the power of intentional choice. After over a decade of working in the cruise industry, I made a sudden shift to a life on land and, after working some time in a corporate job that left me feeling unfulfilled, I decided to make an intentional choice to pursue new educational endeavours in line with my passion for reading and writing. I wanted to align my academic achievements with the level of my professional expertise, to complete my circle of fulfilment.

Being a single mum, as you might imagine, taking such a decision required courage and careful planning, demanding hard work to fund my dreams, while gaining additional skills and networking within the industry. It would be an understatement to say that the transition was challenging, but with determination and persistence and staying true to my values and goals, I eventually managed to attain the academic success I was reaching for, all while continuing my career and raising my son. What started with an intentional choice brought me greater fulfilment, and it got me closer to my life's purpose. This Bible verse accompanied me along the way: 'I can do all things through Christ which strengthens me' (Philippians 4:13). If I was able to undertake this challenge, overcome all the obstacles and successfully come out at the other end, everyone can! I truly believe that. 'And we know that in all things God works for the good of those who love him, who have been called according to his purpose' (Romans 8:28). You do have the power! You owe it to yourself to ignite that spark of greatness, activate the power of intentional choice and trigger your inner ability to create a life that reflects your true self and achieve your own aspirations. Be inspired and motivate yourself to take on the challenge, manage your time effectively and nurture supportive relationships to help you on the path towards the fulfilment of your boldest dreams.

Lifelong learning

The capacity to learn and adapt in a constantly changing environment is critical for personal and professional development. Technological improvements makes lifelong learning (LLL) possible, helping us to access information and develop our abilities throughout life. Our ongoing efforts to improve ourselves and professionalise our abilities can actually make a huge difference in the world around us. I strongly advise people not to rely solely on the years of basic education provided by the traditional schooling system, and rather fine-tune their knowledge as they progress throughout life and as their experiences open up new opportunities for learning. That is how we continually discover ourselves, push back the limitations of what we can achieve, and manage to stay ahead in our careers and open to new paths of growth and development. If we master ourselves in this way, we may potentially discover the higher purpose of our lives, and some of us may make important contributions to society by sharing our knowledge and unique talents.

The concept of lifelong learning extends beyond formal education, and the abundance of online platforms facilitates this, helping millions to enhance their capabilities and advance their careers. The advantage is that it covers a wide range of domains, including but not limited to, self-directed learning, webinars, online courses, master classes, workshops and experiential learning.

It helps being curious, open to new ideas and looking for opportunities to expand your knowledge and skills. It is no secret that I am a big fan of lifelong learning, and one of its key benefits is that it keeps my mind active and engaged all the time. The long-term advantages of constant mental stimulation, proven by neuroscience, is that it improves brain performance while lowering the risk of age-related cognitive decline. We empower our brains by what we feed them, and activities such as reading, writing, learning a new language, playing an instrument or solving crossword puzzles improves mental agility, as supported by research by Craik and Bialystok (2006).

LLL is great for professional development, especially in today's job market in which staying updated with industry trends and acquiring new skills is like oxygen. We all know that, during and after the Covid-19 pandemic, the world of work underwent tremendous transformations, and many lost their jobs while others had to embrace lifelong learning and undertake swift professional reconfiguration. Such an approach to learning brings greater job satisfaction and career success, being better prepared to quickly adapt to changing job requirements, seize new opportunities and remain competitive. The unfortunate events of the pandemic caused the emergence of online learning platforms which designed their services to offer a wide range of courses on various topics, helping millions of people to learn at their own pace and convenience, for a fair price. Whatever stage we may be at in our lives, we can all take advantage of the accessibility of these online learning platforms, which simplify the process of skill development and give us access to a vast range of learning tools from the comfort of our homes. We should draw inspiration from Benjamin Franklin's story, a man who was a lifelong learner and self-taught polymath at a time in history when learning was not an easy undertaking. His curiosity and his commitment to continuous learning and self-improvement is truly something to admire, and he serves as a powerful example of the impact of lifelong learning on personal growth and fulfilment (Isaacson, 2003).

Life compass

Imagine a life without any beliefs or principles, drifting aimlessly without knowing where we're going or what we want to do. If we do not have a moral code to guide us, our choices will be random and poor. This, in turn, will leave us with a constant feeling of emptiness and unhappiness in our life; simply said, not having a strong sense of direction creates confusion and tough choices, damaging our mental health and making it hard to deal with life's challenges. A moral compass is an extremely helpful tool, guiding us to make good choices and live honestly, with meaning. And when we have tough problems to deal with or hard choices to make, having strong values helps us stay focused on what is really important and keeps us from straying onto the path of wrongdoing. A life compass is a metaphor for the internal guidance system we all possess, which helps us to live our lives according to strong principles and ethics. That is why we must align our actions with our values, to obtain that sense of authenticity, and inner peace that brings joy to our life. It is important from a young age to develop and follow a moral compass, because it will guide the decisions we will have to make later on in life, giving us a clear sense of direction and purpose along the journey. But how can we acquire such a state-of-the-art compass, where can we buy one?

Once again, the answer lies in ourselves, and there are a few important things we can do to develop our life compass. Self-reflection is one of them. Taking the time to introspect and understand our own beliefs, passions and goals gives us clarity about what really matters to us and what we hope to accomplish in life. Journaling, meditation and personal evaluations are useful tools that can help us in the process of comprehending where we are and where we want to go. When we have a clear grasp of our values and goals, we can use that information to steer our decisions and actions. A life compass acts as a reference point, just like a lighthouse, if you will, allowing us to charge ahead and avoid being persuaded by external temptations and harmful diversions. You have to set clear and precise objectives and then figure out how you can get there. Goals give direction and drive, allowing us to remain focused on the path ahead of us. It is critical to have a balanced approach in life and strive for quick achievements while working for longer-term goals, in other words, keep the ball rolling while ultimately trying to score. Locke and Latham's (2002) empirical study emphasises the need to set both short-term and long-term goals to stay on track.

Ok, so we set goals and then work hard, but what happens next? When we are focused on giving our best and we are working with determination, we must also keep in mind that it is equally important to regularly assess and revise our objectives to ensure they stay relevant and reachable. We also need to keep in mind that the conditions that surround us are in continuous flux, and it is here that an efficient life compass keeps us adaptable and open to change, re-routing every time it is necessary. In other words, while having a sense of direction is important, it is equally important to remain flexible and amend our course by adjusting the sails of our lifeboat, as needed. We all know how unpredictable life is, and being able to adjust to new situations while remaining loyal to our beliefs and aspirations is critical to our long-term survival and success. Without a doubt, there is a tremendous pressure and a constant battle for our minds, which we may be unaware of, on all levels of our existence. The never-ending assault of information and manipulating diversions makes it difficult to remain grounded and focused on what is genuinely important.

Depression, especially in teens and young adults, unrestrained sexual liberty, the vast proliferation of drugs and alcohol abuse in our society, all this comes with long-term and devastating consequences for individuals and communities, causing suffering that can be difficult to overcome. It is important to educate ourselves and our children about the dangers of any form of dependency in order to prevent further harm. Drugs, alcohol, random unprotected sex, etc are common forms of abuse that people inflict upon others and on themselves with little regard for the serious consequences. Focusing on prevention and getting assistance for people dealing with these difficulties is critical if we are to create a better and safer society. The impact from negative influences might reduce our capacity to cope with obstacles and stay afloat in an ever-declining society. We must try our best to surround ourselves with good and supporting people who inspire us and motivate us to make the best choices for our health and well-being. Addressing these challenges openly and pushing for healthier options encourages us to collaborate with one another and build a culture in which people feel empowered to make great decisions for themselves. Education had been and remains the key, and it must be emphasised in our communities through moral and material support and resources to counteract the destructive effects of any form of abuse.

That is why having a strong life compass is crucial, as it allows us to periodically reflect on our values and goals and ensure we are living in accordance with what truly matters. We may not give it much thought, but each one of us is an active part of the wider world, contributing our bit to the welfare of our society. This battle that our society is struggling with may be won by intentionally deciding to defend our ideals. We all must understand that, even in the midst of great adversity, we can manage life's complexities if we have clarity and firm convictions.

Summary

This chapter has presented insights about the power of example. The transformative importance of mindfulness was illustrated, and we looked at how it can enhance our general state of well-being and our performance. We continued our journey, looking into the elements that make us powerful, studying the importance of understanding and embracing our potential so we can become better equipped for the complexities of the modern world, inspire change and achieve lasting success in all our endeavours. We then spoke about how each one of us can act as a catalyst to enable change and actually make a difference using our own abilities and convictions to drive success and create positive outcomes. The next part of the book will focus on solutions and practical recommendations for how you can harness your power to make a difference in your life, in the teams and organisations within which you work, and the world at large.

PART TWO

THE C.A.R.E. MODEL: CONNECTION, AUTHENTICITY, RE-ENGINEERING, EVOLUTION

Life is an unpredictable adventure, filled with challenges, growth and transformation. It is a journey worth embracing with courage and curiosity. We may develop a fuller and more balanced lifestyle if we actively evaluate and maximise some essential characteristics known as life metrics, which refer to relationships, mental well-being, happiness, physical health, career satisfaction and financial stability, work-life balance and personal growth. All these elements have their role, and it is important to be aware and observant of areas for development and to fine-tune the overall quality of our lives. The C.A.R.E. Model aims to explore these elements of your life, and challenges you to leave your preconceptions behind and set out on a trip that will redefine your understanding of experiential life, culture and the very essence of human connection.

In this second part of the book, you will become familiarised with a transformative strategy designed to inspire you to reach your fullest potential and charge ahead towards achieving your dreams. The goal of the C.A.R.E. Model is also to positively impact the social environment around you, creating good vibes and positive ripple effects in the realm of customer experience. The C.A.R.E. Model stands for Connection, Authenticity, Re-engineering and Evolution, and it offers a holistic approach that integrates personal and professional development aimed at achieving a balanced and fulfilling life that positively influences the teams and the organisations you are part of. The C.A.R.E. Model is designed to be a transformative tool for organisations, teams and individuals, and I invite you to explore how these principles profoundly impact our social environment.

Besides using a set of principles, the C.A.R.E. Model proposes a practical development strategy encouraging continuous growth and improvement, and by adopting this model, a positive and lasting impact is generated on a personal and professional level.

6
The Role Of The C.A.R.E. Model

Our life journey offers many opportunities for profound understanding and exploration, giving us a series of tests and revelations. Every event, whether favourable or unpleasant, adds to the complexity of our personal growth and helps shape who we are. We should consider that hardships often bring the greatest transformations, and it is good to keep in mind that major personal development frequently results from stepping outside your comfort zone and tackling obstacles head on. We should welcome ambiguity and be open to the various possibilities that may arise along the path.

Achieve your utmost potential

One of the primary goals of the C.A.R.E. Model is to help people and teams within organisations to achieve their full potential, resulting in an improved state of well-being that flows into the experience we offer our customers and into our relationships with others. This model is like a roadmap for personal and professional growth as we focus on Connection, Authenticity, Re-engineering and Evolution. Along the path, you will activate your motivation to connect on a more meaningful level, reflect on your principles, improve whatever you do and welcome change and creativity in your life.

At a personal level, you may unlock new levels of self-awareness and the capability to establish new and genuine connections. Living authentically helps create a positive and supportive environment in our communities, each one contributing with our personal gifts and talents. Re-evaluating our habits could provide important hints about how we may optimise our efforts, making room for what we truly need in our life and what we wish to achieve. We must also trust the inner process by which we naturally evolve, which helps us to remain adaptable and open to new opportunities for making our dreams come true.

For organisations, adopting the C.A.R.E. Model may enhance team cohesion and better performance. The model assists organisations to create a culture that values connection and authenticity by fostering a sense of belonging and trust among employees. This is a critical aspect, as, in the long run, it drives higher engagement and productivity. Encouraging continuous learning within the organisation's employees creates the ideal conditions for long-term sustainable success. Re-engineering processes to streamline operations and improve efficiency allows businesses to remain competitive in the market.

The impact on the surrounding social environment

The C.A.R.E. Model highlights the significance of our personal impact and positive influence on our social environment. We are motivated to do good if we connect on a personal level with the people we affect, and this concept is the foundation of empathy. Our actions and behaviours have the power to impact those around us, and this model is designed to help us create a positive effect that ripples out into our communities and beyond. Strengthening real relationships and living truthfully motivates people to emulate this free flow of good energy and implement these values into their own lives. The end result is a culture of openness, trust and support, which gradually spreads and improves into the wider social fabric.

Life re-engineering is crucial for creating social impact. Simply said, we can truly contribute to the progress of society if we continually improve and reinvent ourselves. This proactive attitude helps everyone: ourselves, the companies we work for and the broader communities in which we live.

Enhancing customer experience

Looking more closely at the fabric of human interrelations and considering the realm of customer experience, the C.A.R.E. Model provides insights for creating memorable and impactful interactions which prioritise the customer's needs and emotions. Besides the traditional pillars of communication, accountability, responsiveness and empathy, designing products and services around the customer's needs and preferences creates a sense of trust and loyalty. It is an approach which emphasises the importance of active listening, and when taking ownership of our customers' concerns, it is important to show genuine connection and authenticity. Re-engineering customer service processes to be more efficient and responsive significantly enhances the experience and can be an important differentiating factor in a fiercely competitive market. This, however, cannot be accomplished without feedback, identifying areas for development, and making changes that not only meet, but far exceed, the highest demands of our customers.

There are many practical strategies you can use to improve individuals' general state of well-being, resulting in more productive engagement and better employee satisfaction in the workplace, ultimately resulting in a more refined customer experience. Failure to emphasise employee well-being may lead to increased turnover, less productivity and a lower level of CX. As a result, investing in personnel management techniques enables firms to identify and develop individuals who are capable of leading the organisation through times of uncertainty while also driving innovation. The C.A.R.E. Model is designed to assist both individuals and their organisations to create a more positive and comfortable work environment for the mutual benefit of employees, employers, and ultimately, the customers.

Promoting general well-being

The C.A.R.E. Model encourages a holistic approach to well-being by incorporating physical, mental and emotional health activities into daily living. Connection and Authenticity promote emotional well-being, while Re-engineering and Evolution encourage continuous improvement and resilience throughout life. By implementing the C.A.R.E. Model, you commit to living a more balanced and fulfilling life, as this holistic approach is designed to help you prioritise what truly matters, increasing your chances of attaining satisfaction in all that you do, and improving your happiness and overall well-being.

Summary

In this chapter we browsed the C.A.R.E. Model role as a useful tool that can help you achieve your objectives and make a difference in your community, while also improving customer service at work. We briefly introduced the model's constituent parts of Connection, Authenticity, Re-engineering and Evolution, and explored how they are designed to transform your life perspective and make it more meaningful.

In our ever-changing circumstances, it is easy to become overwhelmed and turn to artificial and temporary coping mechanisms. The stress of work, financial and social pressure and personal duties may have a negative impact on our mental and physical health and quick fixes can seem tempting. The C.A.R.E. Model provides a systematic yet adaptable strategy to overcome these problems while thriving.

7

How Far We Have Come

The last twenty years have brought tremendous changes that have affected everything. New technologies, the internet and social media have greatly affected our identities and how we live our lives, and these innovations, meant to connect us, have also turned our experiences into likes, shares and followers. Without us realising it, social media has transformed us, always comparing our lives to others'. From a psychological viewpoint, this comparison frequently results in feelings of inadequacy and a continuous need for external affirmation. According to Twenge (2017), this has particularly impacted younger generations, causing increased anxiety, depression and a decline in overall well-being.

Psychological problems are on the rise, emphasising the need to be careful in how we interact with social media and make daily attempts to prioritise real-life interactions and experiences above digital validation. If we are not careful about it, the commercialisation of our lives through social media can distort our sense of self-worth. Our well-being suffers when we begin to associate our value with the number of followers we have or the amount of responses our posts receive, and this weakens our self-esteem which can become severely eroded over time. External validation is temporary and empty, leaving us feeling alienated and unhappy, and these platforms depict a polished, idealised image of life that is far from the realities of everyday life. In reality, genuine fulfilment comes from inside, when we accept ourselves for who we are and take life as it really is, allowing ourselves to live each moment at its maximum intensity.

As in everything else, the choice is ours to make, and we can overcome the negative influences of social media if we take the time to build genuine connections and value meaningful relationships above superficial ones. Instead of focusing on gaining followers, we can seek deeper, more meaningful relationships that give genuine support and understanding, and this shift in perspective can help to reduce the negative effects of social media and give us a feeling of true belonging and community.

This is easier said than done, I admit, and there is a constant battle for our minds. We are continually inundated with information influencing us from all sides, and it is critical that we are aware of this and carefully filter what we allow into our thoughts. What we mentally absorb every day, unintentionally or otherwise, actually influences our thoughts and actions, stimulating either progress or destruction in our lives. It is critical that we raise the level of awareness about how social media impacts our mental health, as well as understand the detrimental effects of our digital habits and make deliberate decisions to use social media responsibly. There are a few things we can do here, like setting boundaries, limiting screen time or increasing our filtering ability to select feeds that inspire and uplift us, all of which can help us connect with social media in more positive ways. Simply put, by deliberately controlling how we interact with social media, we will learn to drastically reduce its negative impact on our mental health, and aside from benefitting our own lives, this approach inspires others to interact in more honest and genuine ways, both online and offline.

Devaluing the spiritual aspects of life, I think it's fair to say that people these days prefer success, notoriety and money over spiritual matters in the modern superficial and materialistic world. This makes many people feel disconnected from themselves and the fundamental spiritual concepts that give their life significance, meaning and delight. Choosing to ignore the spiritual side of life prevents us from experiencing what makes life meaningful and valuable, and in the long run, we miss out on our chance to develop into harmonious human beings, keeping us from really experiencing life in an authentic way and making it harder to connect with others.

Let us dig deeper into the significance of this: when we take time to reflect on our lives, we should think of how to live a more purposeful and fulfilling life and help ourselves by feeding our spiritual dimension with faith, hope, love and compassion. We are truly amazing and complex beings! You see, just as a healthy diet is essential for our bodies, our spirituality also needs nourishment, to help us develop that sense of inner peace and fulfilment that transcends material things, giving a higher purpose to our lives. The world would certainly be significantly different if people focused more on *being*, rather than *having*. Let us try a short exercise: I invite you to pause for a short while and think about which one of these two verbs – being or having – better defines your life, pick one and write it down on a piece of paper. Then write the equals sign next to it and take a bit of time to think about how happy and fulfilled you feel in your life at this very moment. Finally, come up with a single word that represents your life and write it on the other side of the equals sign and reflect on it, and whether this is truly you.

Spirituality is the connection to an entity higher than ourselves, and it is an essential component of human existence that is directly linked with our sense of joy and fulfilment and our state of well-being. Spirituality provides guidance and helps us to understand what our position is in the world and what our purpose in life is. However, the modern world undervalues this spiritual component, attributing excessive importance to competing performance and financial or material gain. This frequently causes feelings of inadequacy, emptiness and disconnection from our own selves, diminishing our originality. In fact, this is one of the most profound paradoxes of our time: we live in a world that is connected more than ever before, yet we fail to connect with ourselves, and before we realise it, we become increasingly isolated and lonely despite being continuously surrounded by people. We need to acknowledge that the root cause of this is that we have become spiritually disconnected and we are too focused on the materialistic aspects of life. The spiritual dimension of our human existence had been at the core of our well-being ever since our existence began and it is what truly fulfils us and completes our human experience in this life. Just because the modern world has lost sight of it, we do not have to. We should no longer choose to ignore it, as doing so continues to cause a rupture between us and the essence of who we are as individuals, and, as a society, this deepens the sense of emptiness and creates confusion about who we are and why we are on Earth.

The devaluation of spirituality creates a sense of hopelessness and a lack of purpose; in his work *Man's Search for Meaning*, Viktor Frankl (2006) explains how a life devoid of spiritual significance results in an existential vacuum, a condition of inner emptiness and despair. This gap is really reflected in the rise of mental health illnesses, prolonged sadness and feelings of alienation among people today, disrupting the way we interact with each other and limiting our capacity to connect and develop meaningful relationships. This is why it is so important to nurture an authentic relationship with God, or whichever higher power holds meaning for you – to recalibrate a sense of identity, as a unique and amazing human being destined for greatness in this world. By reconnecting with God and your inner self you make a conscious choice to elevate your existence and allow yourself to find true fulfilment and purpose in everything you do. This connection will enhance your human experience and you will find balance as your heart will be filled with peace and joy. You will see beauty and goodness in everything and everyone, and you will want to live your life authentically, being grateful for the opportunities that come your way. In so doing, you can spread love and positivity to those around you, instead of feeling utterly confused, tired and depressed all the time and unable to help yourself, let alone able to make a difference in someone else's life.

You may be wondering what it really means to enhance your human experience by becoming a more spiritual being. You're on the right track if you're thinking this, so don't worry. The C.A.R.E. Model was created to help and teach you how to integrate spiritual practices into your daily life and gain that ideal sense of purpose and fulfilment. It all starts with being open to reconnect, and you do not have to be a transcendental guru to do that, but simply start by examining your daily routines, goals and priorities to ensure they align with your spiritual beliefs and values. If there is a will, there are ways you can work with yourself to make deliberate decisions on the road to spiritual recovery. For example, one method to attain spiritual well-being is to incorporate regular activities like meditation, prayer and introspection in your daily routines, creating a link between your inner self and the divine, giving you a sense of comfort, calm and purpose. Taking a few moments each day for solitude and spiritual connection helps us strengthen our intuitive guidance, which is so vital in overcoming life's obstacles. This has never been truer than it is today, especially in this noisy, overwhelming world we live in. The Bible highlights it best in Psalm 32:8 reminding us of God's promises, 'I will instruct you and teach you in the way you should go; I will counsel you with my loving eye on you.' Think about it further, perhaps, just like you and me, there are many other people who relate to this and who take steps to seek out spiritual communities and engage with like-minded individuals who share common values and who can provide support, inspiration and a sense of belonging. The spiritual journey is a continuing process of growth and searching for deeper meaning and understanding through prayer, divine connection, studying the word of God, and spending time admiring natural beauty. As we embrace spiritual growth, either alone or joining meditation circles, religious groups or spiritual retreats and various communities, we refine our belief system, integrating spirituality practices into our daily lives and enjoying a more balanced and meaningful life.

Physical and mental well-being

We have seen how important spirituality is in our lives, and another important foundation for a satisfying and productive life is our physical and mental well-being. Unless there are signs that something is way off, we frequently overlook these aspects of our lives, and much has been written about this since the Covid-19 pandemic. We have more in common than we want to admit, whether we like it or not. We all want to be successful in our professional and personal life, and to have plenty of money to provide a safety net for our families. At times it feels easier to give up and allow our problems to overwhelm us, but we might find comfort in knowing that everyone is dealing with difficulties in life. We may often find ourselves consumed by a constant battle of emotions and challenged by life's hurdles, which can sometimes sweep us off our feet into a never-ending downward spiral. These are the times that we have to remember that there are people who care about us and could help us overcome our difficulties, and we should not be ashamed or afraid to reach out for help. Even though each of us is unique, we sometimes forget that we share feelings, difficulties and desires, and while the majority of us may seem to have it all together, in reality we are all challenged in some area of our lives and may become confused at times about how to deal with our problems.

We need to be reminded that the closest available help we have is our family, although sometimes you might feel that you want to protect them from worrying excessively and would rather go and see a counsellor who can maintain a neutral attitude and help steer you in the right direction. Whichever the case may be, it is critical to remember that help is available if we have the courage to seek it. The World Health Organization recommends 150 minutes of exercise a week (2010), together with a balanced diet and an appropriate amount of sleep, to maintain excellent physical and mental health. A strong, healthy body increases energy and immunity to illnesses and so it is important to incorporate in our diet fruits, vegetables and whole grains, and to avoid consuming processed foods and sugary products. Staying hydrated, limiting alcohol usage and having zero tolerance for illegal substance use are important elements in our physical health. Always remember to be relentless in prioritising self-care and making healthy choices for your body and mind.

Mental health and well-being are closely related to the physical health of our bodies. In recent years, stress, anxiety and depression have become a major concern in the health of the general population, affecting the quality of life of millions and threatening the very existence of many. We can improve our mental health and strengthen our resilience in the face of life's adversities by adopting some stress-management tactics, mindfulness, prayer, meditation and relaxation techniques. Science has demonstrated the efficacy of these things in lowering stress (Kabat-Zinn, 1990). There are many efficient solutions people can turn to, and professional help is widely available, however it takes will and determination to make conscious adjustments to our habits and to achieve our health objectives. We must remember to celebrate our accomplishments and feel encouraged to continue making improvements while creating a balance between exercise, work, rest and social events. Building supportive relationships is also important for your mental health; strong social ties offer emotional support and may frequently act as a stress reliever. Engage in community events, volunteer, or simply spend quality time with loved ones to boost your sense of belonging, joy and mental wellness.

Summary

This chapter has provided us with an overview of the current challenges that characterise our world, and we have explored some of the difficulties our society is battling with. We also looked at the importance of spirituality, and at some of the consequences of the moral erosion in society caused by devaluing the spiritual dimension of our lives, and how this affects the way we interact with each other. Finally, we discussed how cultivating mindfulness, prayer and prioritising mental and physical health contributes to a greater state of well-being and a more fulfilling human experience.

8

The C.A.R.E. Model: Connection

In this chapter we explore the first pillar of the C.A.R.E. Model: Connection. It is vital for our mental and emotional health that we build strong, meaningful relationships, especially in a world where it's easy to feel lonely and disconnected. Let's look at seven important aspects to building connections and see how each one can improve your life.

1. Awaken your consciousness

We have been talking about the importance of having a fulfilling and genuine human experience in order to positively contribute to your environment. The first step in making genuine connections is to awaken your consciousness. Allow yourself to expand your awareness and better understand yourself and the world around you. You will notice that you are becoming more conscious, not so self-centred, and you are developing greater empathy and compassion for those around you. Take steps to practise self-reflection and recognise the interconnection of all beings, and this will help you make more thoughtful decisions and become more considerate. Find a moment in your day to sit quietly and reflect on your thoughts, feelings and behaviours. Evaluate them on a regular basis to uncover patterns and opportunities for improvement. Remember, you're your best buddy, after all.

Improving your energy flow and raising your consciousness level can be achieved through meditation. I started this technique to help me cope with feelings of excessive exhaustion I was experiencing. Concentrate on your breathing, clear your thoughts without judgement, and allow yourself to be in the present moment. At first, you may have some difficulty clearing your mind, but after a few sessions, it will become something you look forward to.

Use meditation to increase self-awareness, decrease stress and gain general well-being (Kabat-Zinn, 1990). Engaging with different points of view is also important, so take advantage of the information economy in which we live by reading a lot of books, watching documentaries and attending presentations that challenge your perspectives. Engage with people from diverse backgrounds and cultures, and this will expand your understanding and create empathy, helping you to connect more deeply with others.

TOP TIPS

- **Reflect daily:** Ten minutes each day makes a big difference, so reflect on your thoughts, feelings, decisions and actions; they should be in line with your values.

- **Breathe mindfully:** Focus on your breath for a few minutes to calm your mind.

- **Engage with different perspectives:** books, documentaries and conversations on various topics.

- **Take nature walks:** Take regular technology time-outs and reconnect with nature.

Whatever approach you choose, you must be open and patient, knowing that awakening your consciousness is an ongoing journey, but a rewarding one. As you get a better understanding of yourself and the world around you, it will become simpler to form meaningful connections and positively contribute to your social environment.

2. Rapport, relationships, networking

We are taught from childhood that making friends is good for us and that it helps us build a supporting network. We all need encouragement, inspiration and a pat on the back every once in a while. Whether in our personal or professional lives, it is best to connect with people who share our values. That is why it is so important to use self-reflection and understand your hobbies and passions and to be able to meet others who share your interests. The trick is to be proactive and willing to meet new people, going out and participating in social events. Ask open-ended questions and encourage others to share their stories, and when they do, listen actively, being present in the moment and showing empathy. Relationships are a two-way street, so remember to offer your support to others and don't hesitate to also seek help for yourself when you need it. This way you will create mutually beneficial bonds.

TOP TIPS

- **Socialise and join groups:** Build a network that is aligned with your passions and values.
- **Attend networking events:** Be proactive and outgoing at social gatherings.
- **Follow up:** Stay in touch and create opportunities to connect in future.
- **Be a good listener:** Ask open-ended questions and listen with genuine interest.

Relationships require time to build, but it helps to remember that people with similar interests are generally drawn to each other. The key is to participate in social encounters and join like-minded groups, and in time you will manage to build a strong network.

3. Dare to Care

Caring for others is a human trait that brings joy and fulfilment to both the giver and the receiver. If we are kind and compassionate towards the people around us, we can make a positive contribution in the world. We must consider that love is the common denominator of our existence, and spreading love and kindness is essential. Unfortunately, our world today is in a bad shape, with intolerance and xenophobia causing many conflicts. Besides being shattered by an unprecedented mix of crises in recent years, our world today is ravaged by several wars in different regions, and economic and political turmoil are rife. People have become aggressive towards each other, forgetting that having empathy and acceptance makes a huge difference in understanding and lifting each other up when we need it the most. We each need to dare to care, building trust in one another and creating a more harmonious and supportive society. It starts by being more present in our interactions and considering the verbal and nonverbal cues we receive, acknowledging and validating the other person's perspective with respect and consideration. Daring to care also means putting yourself in another's shoes, trying to understand their perspective and feelings, and thereby building stronger, more trustworthy relationships.

TOP TIPS

- **Practise active listening:** Give your full attention to the speaker, nod and acknowledge them.
- **Make empathy statements:** Understand and care about their perspective.
- **Volunteer:** Engage and expose yourself to different experiences.
- **Reflect on emotions:** Put yourself in the other's shoes, and reflect on their motives and feelings.

Empathy goes beyond a casual encounter, and we should never avoid displaying our humanity, and instead show that we care. This goes a long way to creating a culture of support in our communities. Encourage open communication, provide resources for mental health and well-being and celebrate acts of kindness and compassion. You too can enhance the overall moral well-being of the world around you and create a more supportive and inclusive space for everyone by displaying an empathetic approach to your relationships.

4. My story, His glory

When you connect with your inner spirituality, a myriad of possibilities opens up. Once you establish a timeless connection with the divine source of life, you gain a strong sense of purpose and fulfilment, which cannot compare with anything else in the world. This spiritual connection permeates into every facet of your being, helping you overcome life's problems with confidence and faith. The 'My story, His glory' approach is about life transformation, when you surrender all your troubles to God and venture outside your safe zone into the faith zone, to serve others selflessly. A humble heart and closeness to the divine keeps you grounded on the road of righteousness and more inclined to invest yourself with joy in helping others and living for something higher than yourself. This generates a deep sense of peace and contentment, one that cannot be acquired otherwise. I encourage you to begin exploring your spiritual beliefs today. Whether through prayer or meditation, seek ways to connect with your inner self and the divine. Set time aside each day for spiritual thought and practice, which might range from a few minutes of peaceful meditation to an extended period of prayer or study. Sharing your spiritual journey with others can also be enriching, so join a spiritual community or group where you can discuss your beliefs and experiences. You may also engage with others who share your faith and who can provide support, encouragement and a sense of belonging.

TOP TIPS

- **Daily spiritual practice:** Connect with the divine and inner self in prayer, meditation or reflection.
- **Join a spiritual community:** Participate in a spiritual or religious community.
- **Reflect on your journey:** Find God in your life experiences and challenges, and contribute to the glory of the divine through your actions.
- **Practice and rituals:** Introduce spiritual rituals into your daily routine, light a candle, read sacred Bible texts, and spend time in nature to feel connected with the divine.

Embrace the concept of 'My story, His glory' and reflect on how your own experiences and difficulties might serve a higher purpose. Start thinking of the bigger picture and realise that you are part of a broader social and spiritual narrative, and use that to draw inspiration, motivation and significance from your activities. You have the power to influence things in your society, you just need to remember that spirituality is a profoundly personal path. Be open to discover what resonates with you, and as you strengthen your spiritual connection, you will experience more serenity, purpose and fulfilment in your life. Do your best and God will do the rest!

5. Attitude of gratitude

Having a deep spiritual connection with the divine allows us to appreciate what we have and gain a sense of satisfaction. Adopting a grateful attitude considerably improves our well-being and outlook on life, and concentrating on the positive parts and expressing appreciation for the benefits we have sends a positive message to others. Feelings of joy, resilience and relentless hope are the outcomes of an attitude of gratitude, and it helps to write down three things you are thankful for each day. Whether it is a beautiful sunrise, your and your family members' health, or a personal accomplishment, reflecting on these positive things moves your focus away from what you lack and onto what you have, making you feel substantially better. It is crucially important to incorporate gratitude into your daily routine, so begin and end your day with a prayer of thanksgiving for a more optimistic outlook on life.

TOP TIPS

- **Keep a gratitude journal:** Each day, write down three things you are grateful for.

- **Express appreciation:** Thank those who make a difference in your life, God included.

- **Practise mindful appreciation:** Pause to appreciate the little things, acknowledge and savour these moments.

- **Practice and rituals:** Share things you are grateful for with your family at dinner or reflect on positive moments before bed.

There is a lot of literature on the importance of living in the present moment, appreciating every minute of it and being thankful, and I stand in agreement.

Rather than worrying about the future or dwelling on the past and missing the present moment, we should concentrate on finding fulfilment and joy in a genuine human experience, living life at its fullest, with all its ups and downs. Life is meant to be lived and not idealised from a distance. Live a full, meaningful life, sharing memorable moments with your dear ones, and allow yourself to live in the present as life unfolds.

6. Mindfulness

Closely related to gratitude, mindfulness helps us to be completely present and involved in the moment. It defuses stress and increases attention. You may also enhance your cognitive processes and attain emotional clarity by practising mindfulness, resulting in a more balanced and productive life. Begin adding mindfulness exercises into your everyday routine, such as mindful breathing. You should preferably be in a relaxed setting, but even when you are at the office you can take a few minutes to sit down with your eyes closed and focus on your breath, returning your attention to it any time your mind wanders.

Another effective mindfulness practice is the body scan meditation. Take a few minutes to mentally scan your body from head to toe with your eyes closed, noticing any areas of tension or discomfort and consciously relaxing those areas. This practice helps you become more aware of your physical sensations and experience a well-deserved relaxation. Mindfulness can be readily integrated into your regular activities, so, strive to be completely present.

TOP TIPS

- **Practise mindful breathing:** For a few minutes, inhale deeply, hold your breath, and then exhale slowly.

- **Use the body scan meditation:** Close your eyes and mentally scan your body from head to toe. Consciously relax any areas of tension.

- **Engage in mindful activities:** In everything you do, engage 100%, and focus on sensations.

- **Use mindfulness apps:** Headspace or Calm can guide your practice routine.

---

7. Mental health, well-being

The environment we live in keeps us continually grinding for our livelihood, and we can often find ourselves constantly worrying about what will happen next. It therefore becomes critical to prioritise our mental health and well-being, avoiding tension and negative thought patterns, especially having to worry about things that are beyond our control.

CASE STUDY: Motherhood experience

One of my clients became a parent, and once she returned to work, she was really struggling to balance everything. She came to counselling feeling overwhelmed by the competing demands on her time, feeling burnt out and with a sense of inadequacy in both roles. Together, we reframed her perspective on work-life balance and focused on the quality rather than the quantity of time she spent in each area. We worked to set realistic expectations and priorities, identifying areas where she could delegate or reduce her workload. We implemented time management strategies, which included setting boundaries between work and personal time and incorporating regular self-care practices to help manage stress. The client also learned how to communicate her needs effectively to both her employer and her family, ensuring that she had the support necessary to balance her responsibilities. She managed to find a sustainable rhythm that allowed her to meet her professional obligations without compromising her role as a mum.

You must resort to mindfulness and other techniques to manage stress so you can feel better and happier. Exercising makes you feel happier and more energetic. I suggest finding activities you enjoy and doing them often.

TOP TIPS

- **Get into a self-care routine:** Include activities you enjoy and which relax you (reading, exercising, gardening, cooking or simply having a long soak in a foamy bath).

- **Seek support:** Call on friends, family or professionals, and talk about your feelings and challenges.

- **Practise stress management:** Use mindfulness, meditation and physical activity to boost your mood and energy levels.

- **Seek professional help:** A therapist or counsellor can provide guidance and support tailored to your specific needs.

- **Find a work-life balance:** set clear boundaries to ensure time for relaxation, hobbies and social activities.

You are not neglecting anyone if you prioritise your mental well-being, enhancing your resilience, productivity and the overall quality of your life. If you are not well, your ability to help anyone else is severely affected, and it is absolutely fine to ask for help and take care of yourself.

Summary

In this chapter, we explored the first pillar of the C.A.R.E. Model – Connection. We learned that by awakening our consciousness, building rapport and relationships, practising empathy, nurturing our spiritual connection, adopting an attitude of gratitude, cultivating mindfulness and prioritising our mental health, each one of us can have meaningful connections that magnify our personal and professional lives. These practical tips will contribute to your fulfilment while enhancing the well-being of your social environment.

9
The C.A.R.E. Model: Authenticity

Nowadays, it has become tough to be honest and true to oneself. The pressures of society force you to conform and meet certain standards, but you must not let yourself be changed. Keeping true to oneself is important for personal development and authenticity, but it is a costly quality. I say costly because it requires sacrifice and vulnerability, which may be difficult to sustain in a culture that frequently prioritises conformity over originality. Social media increases the pressure to conform and portray a controlled version of oneself to the public, making authenticity even more difficult to accomplish. But it is important to remember that being authentic makes you a valuable human being, and is worth the cost, because it helps you find those few genuine friends who surround you with a sense of fulfilment that cannot be achieved through a facade. Authenticity is about accepting your true self and living in accordance with your values and beliefs. This chapter will go over practical strategies to help you celebrate your individuality, trust yourself, see failure as an opportunity, honour your own beliefs, tap into your creativity, discover intrinsic drive, and perceive rejection as a sort of divine redirection.

1. Celebrating your uniqueness

We have established that everyone is uniquely created. There is no one like you in the entire world – there has never been and there will never be another person exactly like you on this planet. The sooner you realise and internalise that, the faster you can get on your path of discovery. It is important to embrace your individuality and treat yourself with the gift of love. Being real and living your truth is powerful. You must fight to gain the courage to be authentic and follow your own path with confidence. This way you are sure to leave your mark in the world in your own unique way.

Recognising and accepting our differences is the most critical step towards celebrating our uniqueness. Our individual similarities and disparities give rise to unimaginable variations of possibilities, and creation is truly remarkable in that way – there is divine beauty in everyone and intelligence in the world's design and it should be regarded as such. Each of us has a unique set of experiences, abilities and perspectives that shape who we are, and it is essential to accept and respect our differences and express ourselves honestly, as well as living with purpose and integrity.

TOP TIPS

- **Self-reflect:** What makes you unique? What strengths and passions do you possess? What experiences have shaped your perspective? Write these down and remind yourself of them regularly.

- **Express yourself:** Express your unique qualities through your work, your hobbies or your personal style, and embrace your own uniqueness.

- **Surround yourself with support:** Celebrate your uniqueness, but join groups or communities that share some of your similarities.

You must examine your personal and professional personas to find your strengths and limitations, and then seek to maximise your potential in both areas. Be aware of your differences and accept them as distinct characteristics that distinguish you from others, making you special. Consider whether your career serves a greater purpose. This might help you align with your genuine self. Consider how your employment benefits you, others, and society as a whole. A strong sense of purpose is a powerful motivator in your job, and every one of us plays an important part in making the world a better place just by contributing our unique abilities and views.

TOP TIPS

- **Identify your values:** Identify your important values and consider how your job aligns with these values.
- **Seek meaning:** Find meaning in your work, take projects that align with your values, and choose roles that have a positive impact.
- **Make changes if needed:** If your values do not match your professional role, be bold and make changes.

Here is something important to consider when you think about your life: the world is waiting for your light to shine brightly, so do not deprive it of your brilliance, and fire up your motivation engines to let your authentic self radiate with confidence and passion.

2. Trust yourself

We have all experienced frightening situations, crunch times, when we felt confused and doubted our ability to conquer our problems. At these moments, we must dig deep and believe in our resilience and strength to persevere. It is necessary to understand yourself before you can trust yourself. Allow plenty of time to explore your ideas and feelings, likes and dislikes, as well as to gain confidence in your own talents and decisions. Trust your instincts and believe that you know what is best for you – this is vital for guiding you through moments of confusion and doubt. Believing in yourself and your talents is critical in order to keep going and to achieve your goals, especially in difficult conditions when you are being put to the test.

TOP TIPS

- **Use affirmations:** Boost your self-confidence. Reinforce your self-belief, by repeating 'I trust myself' or 'I am capable and strong'.

- **Reflect on past successes:** Remember your achievements and remind yourself of your good decisions.

- **Listen to your inner voice:** Trust your inner voice and your instincts, and take a moment to listen to your gut feelings.

- **Practise decision-making:** Build confidence by making decisions regularly and boost your confidence in your ability to trust yourself.

---

3. There is no such thing as failure

During times of difficulty and adversity, our endurance and faith is tried in ways that some of us cannot begin to imagine, but it is critical to remain firm in your beliefs and never give up on your objectives. You must remind yourself that there is no such thing as failure, there is only the possibility to progress from the situation you are facing, which will eventually lead to something better. If you want to live truly, you must view setbacks as learning opportunities. It is tempting to perceive failure as a setback, but you must make an intentional effort to avoid this and consider it a learning experience that will help you get closer to your ultimate goals.

CASE STUDY: Overcoming procrastination

We all experienced at some point procrastinating in our tasks. In this instance, despite having a strong enthusiasm for his profession and clear goals, a client found himself frequently delaying key tasks, resulting in stress and a sense of underachievement. This impediment was impeding his progress at work, and it was undermining his self-confidence, generating a great deal of worry and concern. We therefore developed a strategy consisting of time management techniques and cognitive behavioural techniques to address the root causes of his procrastination. We identified some of his underlying concerns and his fixation on perfectionism that were driving his behaviour, and we reframed them. I helped him break down chores into smaller, more manageable stages and create a daily routine that prioritised his most critical duties. We also introduced some accountability measures, such as having him check in with me once a week to report on his progress and discuss any issues.

Over several months, he actively followed these recommendations and his procrastination diminished. He adopted a more systematic approach in his job, which increased his productivity and reduced much of the stress he was initially struggling with. When we last met, he was more confident in his ability to achieve his goals.

We must remind ourselves that there is no such thing as failure, only feedback and opportunities for progress, which, after some work, will eventually lead to success. We learn, grow, and become stronger people by persevering through these problems, and if the so-called 'mistakes' never happened, we would not have the chance to evolve and improve at what we do.

TOP TIPS

- **Reframe failure:** Change your perspective on failure – view it as a valuable lesson that provides insight and growth.

- **Learn from your mistakes:** Analyse what went wrong and what you can learn.

- **Celebrate effort:** Remember to recognise and celebrate the effort you have put in.

- **Stay resilient:** Develop resilience by staying positive and persistent.

What you need to take away from this is that perceiving failures as stepping stones to success rather than hurdles helps us create resilience and attain our full potential. It is therefore critical that we accept difficulties and push ourselves to step outside our familiar comfort zone to achieve new heights of personal development.

4. Personal values and beliefs

A common practice in life coaching and personal development counselling is undertaking the personal values and beliefs test, as it highlights essential elements of who we are. It is of significance because it influences our decisions and actions in many areas of life. To live a fulfilled and true life, you must be willing to be intentional and honestly look at your inner self, and then reflect on and comprehend your beliefs. Personal values and beliefs include integrity, honesty, respect, family, spirituality, equality and personal growth, as well as kindness, creativity, courage, appreciation and generosity, etc. They help shape who we are, as they drive our thoughts and actions, mapping the course of our existence through life.

TOP TIPS

- **Identify your values:** Identify your core values and principles to guide your actions.
- **Evaluate your actions:** Evaluate your actions and decisions.

- **Set boundaries:** Set boundaries, communicate them clearly, and stick to them.
- **Live with integrity:** Strive to live with integrity.

Throughout life, alignment is essential to attaining a balance between our moral compass and our actions, guiding our decisions and the behaviours that we display every day. Previously, in more deeply religious societies, the decalogue (the Ten Commandments) served as life-guiding principles, but nowadays society promotes a culture that encourages the dilution of these values, blurring them and making it difficult at times to differentiate between good and bad and make the right choices. To live authentically means to live in harmony and have a strong set of values and express ourselves with conviction. This means matching our actions with our values and beliefs, and making decisions that represent who we really are and what we stand for.

5. Creativity/originality

Creativity is a key component of expressing our true selves and is what gives originality its unique spark. What does it take to make you who you are, and set you apart from others? Creativity makes our life resourceful, interesting and colourful, and we must have the courage to explore our creativity and uniqueness and express ourselves in original ways by developing inventive solutions to the problems we confront.

TOP TIPS

- **Explore new interests:** Try new activities and explore different interests.

- **Design a creative space:** Designate a space in your home for creativity.

- **Take risks:** Try new things and embrace opportunities.

- **Collaborate with others:** Share ideas to gain new perspectives and find innovative solutions.

We must never underestimate the power of our creativity and imagination, especially if we are well connected, in synergy with nature, the divine and the people around us. We must draw motivation from hardships and use creative ways to better ourselves and build our lives in authentic ways. Nobody can be you better than yourself – this is a precious lesson to keep close to your heart.

6. Intrinsic motivation

Some of us are parents and know only too well the challenges of getting children to do something they don't want to do, such as chores or homework. We may often manage to motivate or cajole them into action, but imagine how amazing it would be if, one day, you returned home from work and they had done their homework and cleaned their room without being told to do so. Intrinsic motivation, an extensively researched topic, is the will to act for personal contentment rather than for external incentives, which depends solely on each individual. The things we do when we think that no one's watching are also rooted in intrinsic motivation. We all have intrinsic motivation and, at the end of the day, it all boils down to our unique personalities and what actually drives us to do the things we do, in the way we chose to do them. Intrinsic motivation is responsible for the amazing things one achieves throughout life without being told, and it is the element that transforms goals and aspirations into quantifiable results. It is more potent and long-lasting than extrinsic motivation because it comes from within, from our passions and ambitions, which are tied to our life purpose and dreams. Overall, motivation is essential for obtaining success and personal fulfilment in life, and it is the driving force that propels people to work hard and endure in the face of adversity. Intrinsic motivation has limitless potential, and its benefits are worth fighting for: greater personal well-being and happiness, creativity, and a general sense of fulfilment.

TOP TIPS

- **Identify your passions:** Incorporate passions into work and daily life.
- **Set meaningful goals:** Align meaningful goals with your values.

- **Find joy in the journey:** Focus on joy and satisfaction, and celebrate small victories.
- **Stay true to yourself:** Stay true to your values and passions, and remember that true fulfilment comes from within.

7. Rejection is the ultimate signpost towards divine redirection

Nobody likes rejection. It is painful to deal with as it brings confusion and despair. Nevertheless, it is sometimes needed for us to be rerouted towards the right track. To help ourselves, we may find encouragement in remembering that rejection is not a reflection of our worth, but rather a stepping stone towards something better. We must understand it as a redirection and reframe it as a necessary divine intervention, an opportunity to find a new path that is better suited for us.

If you know you've done everything within your power and have given 100%, that is a battle well fought; leave it in God's hands and rest assured that your best interest is being looked after. However, if things do not evolve in the direction you had planned, you must have faith in the divine plan and trust the process, using rejection as a source of motivation to keep fighting and pursuing our dreams, believing that after rejection, after we have endured for a while, fulfilment awaits. This could well be our chance to actually discover our true purpose in life.

TOP TIPS

- **Reframe rejection:** Remind yourself that rejection is divine redirection towards something better suited for you.

- **Reflect on the experience:** Reflect on what you can learn from the rejection you have experienced.

- **Stay positive:** Keep a positive attitude that is focused on long-term goals.

- **Keep moving forward:** Stay resilient and keep moving forward.

Summary

This chapter has discussed important aspects of the second pillar of the C.A.R.E. Model: Authenticity. We've seen how we may live more honestly and match our behaviours with our inner self by appreciating our individuality, trusting ourselves, considering failure as an opportunity and honouring our own beliefs. We learned that it is essential to give wings to our creativity and have the courage to discover our intrinsic drive, and when things are not perhaps the way we imagined, we must try our best to perceive rejection as a divine redirection. This approach will increase our inner joy and fulfilment, while also helping us to create a more authentic, supportive, and connected society.

10
The C.A.R.E. Model: Re-Engineering

In this chapter we will focus on the third pillar of the C.A.R.E. Model – Re-engineering. It will deconstruct the concept of re-engineering and some of its pre-requisites will be analysed in order to fully understand its potential benefits and challenges. It will look at how re-engineering benefits both businesses and individuals, and some of the concepts discussed highlight how processes and performance may be effectively improved. Re-engineering refers to reassessing and redesigning processes to achieve dramatic improvements in critical performance. In other words, it is important, every once in a while, to reconstruct certain systems and habits to achieve better outcomes and higher levels of efficiency. Let us explore seven essential elements that help to effectively re-engineer various aspects of business and life.

1. Perception

Think of a perception as the lens through which we view the world and understand things that happen to us from our own personal angle. From both a business and a personal perspective, it is important to determine how we approach life's challenges and opportunities. The importance of perception cannot be understated; if it is ignored, confusion and misunderstandings may occur. Therefore, we owe it to ourselves to know how essential it is to have an accurate perception of events, even if sometimes this may mean taking a step back to reassess the situation at hand and evaluate the circumstances objectively. Let us imagine that you are an artist stepping back to look at your unfinished painting from a slight distance. This new perspective allows you to see the bigger picture, identify areas that need improvement and appreciate what you have already accomplished.

What would you change in your business or life? Pause for a minute and think about it. Then, just like the artist, begin the process of re-engineering by identifying key areas that need to be re-designed. If you are an entrepreneur, it might be a department within your organisation, or a manager may think of a certain process that should be re-designed, and his team is responsible for its smooth operation. On a personal level, it might be an important relationship that needs work, or your health or personal development. The first step is to reflect on your objectives, values and current strategies. Take the appropriate actions to determine whether there are conflicts and, if they are not aligned, spend time considering what you can do about it.

TOP TIPS

- **Self-reflection:** Reflect and write down your thoughts and observations about areas to improve.

- **Seek feedback:** In business, ask for customers' feedback. In your personal life, speak to trusted friends, family members or colleagues.

- **SWOT:** Review your Strengths, Weaknesses, Opportunities and Threats in your personal and professional lives.

- **Mindfulness practice:** Incorporate meditation and journaling to enhance clarity.

---

2. Success mindset

Earlier, we saw how a success mentality is directly linked with a positive and proactive approach to accomplishing your objectives. It is essential to believe in yourself and be prepared to take the required efforts to achieve your goals.

Let us consider the following analogy: think of a success mentality like the foundations of a skyscraper. Just as these solid foundations support the towering structure, a success mindset provides us with the support, inspiration and motivation we need to work towards our dreams and achieve amazing things. Cultivating confidence in your talents and having a good attitude in the face of adversity is what distinguishes successful people from the others. It does not imply that you are disregarding challenges, but rather that you are taking a proactive approach with resilience and resolve. Setting clear goals, visualising success and taking consistent action towards achieving those goals is a key factor in achieving success.

TOP TIPS

- **Set clear goals:** Define clear, achievable goals that align with your values.

- **Visualisation:** Mentally rehearse achieving your goals.

- **Positive affirmations:** Reinforce a success mindset and boost self-belief.

- **Continuous learning:** Stay committed to learning and self-improvement.

---

3. Resilience

Trying times have a way of demonstrating the need to keep a positive mental attitude and maintain an optimistic perspective to be able to successfully pivot and adjust to change when going through difficult times. Over the last several years, our resilience has been severely tested by a variety of crises such as the 2008 financial crisis, the Covid-19 outbreak and, currently, the geopolitical tensions and wars in many parts of the world which have been keeping us on a constant state of alert. It is in times of crisis that we develop evolving strategies, so remember to maintain a positive attitude and seek support when you need it. The important thing is that we need to stay focused on our objectives and be strong and resilient in the face of adversity. This way we keep moving forward and strive to do the right thing, regardless of what difficulties life may throw at us. Keep in mind that, just as gold is polished in the fire, so are we refined by life's challenges. A person's strength is truly defined by their capacity to rapidly recover from adversity and hardships and shine brighter than before.

> **TOP TIPS**
> - **Develop coping strategies:** Practise coping strategies such as deep breathing exercises, prayer, meditation or physical activity.
> - **Connect to a support network:** Seek out encouragement and advice when facing challenges.

- **Practise gratitude:** Reflect on the positives, keep a gratitude journal to help you shift the focus from challenges to blessings.
- **Stay flexible:** Be open to change and willing to adapt. Flexibility is key to resilience.

The analogy of resilience as a rubber band that can stretch and flex without breaking has been much contested. The bottom line is that resilience enables us to bear life's demands and failures by gaining mental and emotional strength to overcome obstacles and emerge stronger. Resilient people look at problems as chances for growth rather than as overwhelming obstacles, and they maintain a positive attitude by framing failures as learning experiences and opportunities to improve and adapt.

4. Relentlessness

It is no insignificant thing that, after having suffered for a while, we tend to emerge stronger and more resilient, but when this suffering befalls us again and again, we have two options: we either collapse, helpless, or we fight, hopeful. The latter option makes us develop an unbeatable inner strength that can withstand even the toughest of situations. This is relentlessness at its finest. It is a committed drive to following your goals despite the hurdles, which necessitates perseverance, devotion and a steadfast unwillingness to give up. Sometimes, we have to burn all the boats and charge ahead with all thy might. Never give up on your dreams. If you give up on your dreams, you are giving up on you. My respect goes to the grinding husband who works double shifts to provide for his family, or the marathon runner fighting through tiredness and suffering to cross the finish line, or the single mums or dads working hard to raise and educate their children or the student who goes to work after classes – it is their unwavering commitment and relentlessness that drives the greatest achievements. You, too, have to be relentless and continue to grind persistently, focused on your objectives and pushing forward with unwavering determination, even when the going gets tough, and the tough gets tougher.

TOP TIPS

- **Stay focused:** Keep goals at the forefront of your mind, and remember your purpose and your *why*.
- **Break it down:** Break your goals into smaller, more manageable tasks.
- **Celebrate progress:** Acknowledge and celebrate progress along the way.
- **Stay positive:** Keep a positive attitude and believe in your ability to succeed.

Remember that relentlessness necessitates a strong sense of purpose and dedication. So set high expectations for yourself and be prepared to put in the hard work and effort required to attain your goals. You can do it!

5. Framing crisis

Throughout our lives, we are bombarded by all kinds of difficulties, and it is beneficial to frame crises as opportunities and to consider our problems as important learning experiences. In a business setting, complaints, much like personal life issues, can provide useful insights and motivate progress. Consider a front desk clerk who is approached by a customer with a complaint. While the situation may not be easy to handle, if managed correctly, the issue can be transformed into an opportunity to improve the experience for future customers. It is therefore important to perceive crises and complaints as gifts allowing us the opportunity to develop and progress. Complaints frequently highlight areas for improvement which may have gone unnoticed. If they are received with gratitude and resolved proactively, performance will be enhanced and so is the customer's overall experience, which creates a stronger connection and builds long-term loyalty.

TOP TIPS FOR YOURSELF
- **Reframe challenges:** Reframe crises as an opportunity to learn and grow.
- **Seek feedback:** Welcome feedback and view complaints as constructive feedback.
- **Develop problem-solving skills:** Enhance your skills, brainstorm, use critical thinking and decision-making.

- **Stay calm:** Maintain composure, take deep breaths and stay focused.

TOP TIPS FOR ORGANISATIONS

- **Prepare for emergencies:** Have contingency plans and procedures. Regularly train your staff on emergency management.
- **Communicate effectively:** Maintain clear communication, provide information and updates to all stakeholders.
- **Stay organised:** Keep records and documentation of any incidents or situations that arise, and your response efforts.
- **Learn and improve:** After an incident/situation, conduct a thorough review to enhance crisis-management procedures.

6. Crisis management

Am I right in saying that many of us have been faced with a situation that has required us to think fast and make quick decisions? Some of us, perhaps, experience this on a daily basis. Everyone goes through a similar situation at some point in their lives. If you felt like me, that was perhaps when you saw yourself helpless and vulnerable, but it is also when you may have discovered your true strength and potential. It is important to be able to adapt to unexpected challenges and communicate effectively in stressful situations. In our work environments especially, we need to develop our crisis-management skills in order to manage these situations effectively. Effective management means to prepare for, to respond to and recover from, crises.

CASE STUDY: A medical emergency

One of the elder guests on a cruise ship had an unfortunate medical emergency. At the time she was on the lido deck, nowhere near the medical facility or close to any of her family members, and the crew members that were there at the time handled the situation with professionalism and efficiency. They quickly assessed what was going on, called for immediate medical care to be provided, and communicated with the family. The situation had the potential to degenerate into a tragic situation, but the crew members' rapid response and effectiveness turned it into a happy ending. Like many other unpredictable situations that happen on a daily basis aboard cruise ships, this crisis highlighted the importance of having well-trained staff and clear procedures in place.

TOP TIPS FOR YOURSELF

- **Stay calm and prioritise:** Maintain composure, think clearly, identify urgency, prioritise.

- **Communicate:** Reach out for help, use clear and concise communication, concentrate on what you can control.

- **Practise self-care and stay flexible:** Eat, sleep, take breaks, avoid burnout, be ready to adjust as needed.

- **Reflect:** Evaluate your crises and learn from them.

TOP TIPS FOR ORGANISATIONS

- **Identify risks:** Use risk assessments to identify potential crises, consider natural disasters, financial challenges, health emergencies, etc.

- **Crisis plan:** Make sure you have comprehensive crisis-management plans for different types of emergencies.

- **Train:** Train your team on response procedures and conduct simulations.

- **Communicate:** Communicate plans and expectations clearly with all stakeholders.

- **Evaluate and improve:** Evaluate your responses, identify improvements, and update your crisis management plans.

Remember the three Rs, whether in individual cases or in organisational responses to crisis. Effective crisis management involves these three key phases:

- **Research:** Identify potential risks and develop contingency plans.

- **Response:** Take immediate action to mitigate the impact of the crisis/situation.

- **Recovery:** Learn from the experience and fine-tune your procedures.

7. Fail to plan or plan to fail

Planning is an essential part of achieving success and overcoming difficulties. It all starts with drafting an idea, a strategy, and then adjusting it along the way when analysing progress, and repeating the process if successful. These are all crucial components of continuous growth.

Imagine you want to get married and, together with your future spouse, you show up at church without any prior arrangements. You may get sad and waste time, but you only have yourself to blame for not planning this event. In this way, failing to plan creates confusion and missed opportunities. On a personal level and in organisations, planning provides direction and helps us stay on the path towards our goals, so the first step is to set those clear objectives, outline the steps to achieve them and identify any potential obstacles. When implementing the plan, consider making changes and whatever necessary adjustments along the way. Equally important is to evaluate and regularly review your progress, along with making improvements. Then all you have to do is to repeat the process, ensuring continuous growth and success.

TOP TIPS

- **Set clear objectives:** Define clear, specific and achievable goals. Break them down and create a detailed plan.

- **Implement your plan:** Take action, be proactive, adaptable, make adjustments as needed.

- **Evaluate progress:** Review progress in relation to your goals. Organisations can use metrics and feedback to assess and identify areas for improvement.

- **Aim for continuous improvement:** Make improvements to the plan, and stay committed to continuous learning.

- **Stay flexible:** Be willing to adapt your plan as needed – flexibility is key.

Summary

In this chapter, we've explored the third pillar of the C.A.R.E. Model – Re-engineering. We learned that you can truly transform your life by assessing your current situation, adopting a success mindset, building resilience, staying relentless, framing crises as opportunities, managing crises effectively and planning for success.

You may actually re-engineer many elements of your life and work to achieve better results. These practical tools promote personal and professional development, while they may also put you on the path to reaching your life goals, encouraging a more resilient and flexible response to life's problems.

11

The C.A.R.E. Model: Evolution

In this chapter, we take a look at the final pillar of the C.A.R.E. Model: Evolution. The environment that surrounds us can easily draw us into debilitating routines that we cannot escape from. This can create a limiting belief system that we may cling onto, preventing us from becoming the best version of ourselves. Come to think about it, how many times in our lives have we had to return over and over to the same issue that never seems to go away? This is a common struggle many of us battle with, but either through counselling or self-awareness and deliberate choices, we may break away from these cycles and embrace personal progress.

This chapter discusses seven fundamental aspects related to facing adversities and emerging stronger on the other side. We can only appreciate the pleasure of a transformed life if we strive for perfection and constantly evolve with perseverance and grace.

1. Human experience is evolving – are you part of the process?

As we go through life, our outlook and experiences change, and, unfortunately, this change is not always for the better. Although it can be extremely challenging to grow in a continuously changing world, we must remain committed and work tirelessly to developing ourselves. Personal growth and development are basic components of the human experience that are always changing due to a number of external factors. For starters, technological innovation has forced the world into a rapid pace of development, altering the way we live and work over the past several decades. This means it is more important than ever to keep the pace and adapt. The internet, along with digital technologies, has revolutionised the way people around the world communicate and interact in relation to all aspects of our lives, including matters of health, trade, business, education and commerce. Global events, economic fluctuations and environmental crises further underscore the need for adaptability. Such changes can disrupt our lives, but they also present opportunities for growth and innovation, and only if we develop resilience and a growth mindset, can we navigate these challenges and emerge stronger.

TOP TIPS

- **Commit to lifelong learning:** Enrol on courses, attend workshops, read, stay curious and open to new knowledge and experiences.

- **Develop your skills:** Identify skills relevant to your goals and invest time developing them.

- **Embrace diversity:** Engage with diverse cultures and perspectives, travel and participate in cultural events.

- **Stay informed:** Keep up with global trends and events, understand the broader context, and make better-informed decisions.

- **Reflect and adapt:** Reflect on your experiences, identify areas for growth, and adapt your strategies and goals.

2. Embrace challenges as opportunities

Our outlook in life has a major effect on the way we face problems. It can influence whether we perceive them as challenges that can and must be overcome, or we can see them as overwhelming obstacles. Embracing problems as opportunities is a perspective that may change the way we face barriers in life. Challenges are unavoidable, but recognising them as chances for progress allows us to accomplish significant personal and professional development. This adjustment in our mentality enables us to identify opportunities for learning and progress in every challenging scenario.

When you're feeling down and lacking in drive, look at other people who are less fortunate than you, or draw inspiration from those who inspire us. Take, for example, the story of Thomas Edison, who failed hundreds of times before successfully developing the electric light bulb, or the example we used earlier of JK Rowling, who suffered multiple setbacks before finding a publisher for her books. Instead of viewing your failures as setbacks, gather all your strength, hope, faith and ability and continue to grind until you get closer to your desired accomplishment. This perseverance and dedication demonstrates the potential of perceiving problems as opportunities.

TOP TIPS

- **Reframe challenges:** Change your perspective and view challenges as opportunities.
- **Set goals:** Set specific goals, break the challenge into manageable steps and focus on making progress.
- **Seek support:** Ask for help, advice and support when you need it.
- **Celebrate small wins:** Celebrate small victories along the way, and recognise the progress you have made.
- **Reflect on lessons:** Reflect on the experience you have gathered.

---

3. Continuous uncertainty

Life is all about a perpetual state of change. In fact, as we all know, change is the only thing that remains constant, and, similar to our ancestors throughout history, we are also obliged to adjust to ever-changing conditions in order to thrive in today's society.

TOP TIPS

- **Stay flexible:** Let go of rigid plans and embrace change.

- **Plan for contingencies:** Use contingency planning and rehearse how you might respond in different scenarios.

- **Stay informed:** Keep up with trends, stay informed, anticipate changes and adapt accordingly.

- **Practise resilience:** Build resilience, practise self-care, exercise, prayer and meditation, and spend time with loved ones.

- **Embrace learning:** View change as opportunity to grow, develop new skills and gain knowledge.

---

4. Engagement: It is enough for good men to do nothing

We have a moral obligation to each other to stand up for what is right and join human rights organisations in a collaborative effort to make a difference in the lives of those who cannot do so by themselves. We can all make a difference and choose to light up the darkness, making positive changes in our society, one small step at a time. Active engagement can take many forms: volunteering and community service, affiliation with professional organisations and participation in social movements. Take into consideration that engaged individuals are often seen as leaders and role models, inspiring others to take action and contribute to the greater good, so get engaged in as many activities as you can! While you are preoccupied with making a difference in the society you live in, though, make sure you reserve time to be present in your personal and professional life, as well. Be caring and provide for your family, and be productive at work. Fulfilment comes from being engaged and joining the causes you believe in.

TOP TIPS

- **Get involved:** Get involved, volunteer, donate, join community groups or nonprofit organisations.

- **Take the initiative:** Do not wait, make a positive impact today, take initiative and lead the way.

- **Be present:** Be fully present in all your interactions and activities – listen attentively, participate actively, show genuine interest.

- **Advocate for change:** Use your voice to advocate for good causes you believe in, participate in *peaceful* protests, raise awareness through social media.

- **Reflect on impact:** Reflect on the impact of your actions, consider how you can make a positive difference in your community and beyond.

5. Energy

Most of us have a friend whose energy and positivity lights up the room when they come in. These people inspire us to have a different outlook on life and spread joy around us. But you also can be that friend for someone else. Energy is the driving force behind all our actions, it fuels our motivation, creativity and perseverance. A good understanding of effective energy management helps you increase productivity in your busy days and feeds your well-being. Energy comes from various sources, especially from a good state of physical health, mental clarity and emotional balance, and it can be shared freely with others. If you're looking to improve your energy levels, you can do so through a nutritious diet, plenty of exercise and good quality sleep.

In professional settings, energy management is crucial for sustaining performance and avoiding burnout, and it helps to recognise your peak energy times and schedule important tasks during these periods to enhance productivity.

TOP TIPS

- **Prioritise sleep and have a healthy diet:** Aim for between seven and nine hours of quality sleep, a diet rich in fruits, vegetables, lean proteins and whole grains, stay hydrated and avoid excessive caffeine and sugar.

- **Regular exercise and stress management:** Get plenty of physical activity and exercise to boost energy levels, use stress-management techniques, and use mindfulness, prayer and meditation for emotional balance and mental clarity.

- **Energy peaks:** Identify your peak energy times and schedule important tasks during these periods.

- **Set clear goals and develop a routine:** Break down goals into smaller tasks. Your daily routine should incorporate time for work, exercise, rest and personal development.

- **Stay organised and seek inspiration and motivation:** Use tools like planners, to-do lists, or digital apps to keep track of tasks and deadlines, have a clear plan for reaching your objectives, surround yourself with positivity, read, look at motivational content and engage in a supportive community.

- **Network and stay flexible:** Adapt your plans as needed. Cultivate the flexibility to overcome obstacles and adjust strategies without losing momentum, build relationships, and find new opportunities, insights and support through networking.

Remember that having daring dreams and ambitions can fuel your energy and drive towards progress. It is an incredible source of energy since it is derived from intrinsic motivation, which inspires you to put in the effort and accomplish your goals. Igniting your interests and objectives may actually feed your energy and desire for success, making the possibilities limitless.

6. Excellence

It is quite probable that you have felt the pressure to succeed in your work and I know exactly how overwhelming it can be. Excellence is tough to attain, especially in such an overly competitive world, but it is an ideal that inspires us to keep pushing forward. We must work hard and try to meet high performance requirements while delivering excellent outcomes. Without a relentless commitment to continuous improvement, attention to detail and a dedication to doing our best in everything, excellence remains just a dream. Don't get me wrong, excellence is not about being perfect, but about giving your absolute best and learning from every experience. Besides perseverance, discipline and a growth mindset, it requires setting high expectations for yourself, and delivering those standards.

TOP TIPS

- **Set high standards:** Clearly define your high standards for your work and personal life, and strive to meet or exceed them consistently.

- **Strive for continuous improvement:** Commit to learning, seek feedback and take action to enhance skills and performance.

- **Pay attention to the details:** Pay attention to the details in your work, and always ensure accuracy and precision.

- **Stay disciplined:** Develop disciplined habits and routines.

- **Celebrate achievements:** Remember to reflect on and acknowledge your achievements.

---

7. Enhancing the human experience (lighting up the darkness)

We are more alike than we like to admit, but one thing we have in common is that we each have the ability to make a change in the world, and we should never undermine that power. We are uniquely gifted, and it is our choice to share those gifts with the world. We have a moral duty to reflect upon our inner being and identify the gifts hidden in us, and we can then perfect and fine-tune them to a high level of professionalism and put them to use for the benefit of our society. In this way, everyone contributes their natural abilities to the advancement of civilisation. In other words, every one of us has been given an undeniable mandate to contribute to the well-being of our planet by illuminating the darkness around us and improving the human experience. We may achieve success in this global mission by doing acts of kindness, compassion and creativity that are targeted at improving the lives of others by fostering a more inclusive and supportive culture.

TOP TIPS

- **Do acts of kindness:** Perform random acts of kindness. Small gestures cause a big impact and ripple positivity into the world around us.

- **Volunteer:** Dedicate time to volunteer for causes you care about – your efforts can truly make a difference.

- **Innovate for good:** Use your skills and creativity to develop solutions to social challenges.

- **Promote well-being:** Support initiatives to promote mental health and well-being.

- **Foster empathy:** Encourage empathy and understanding, and show compassion.

- Try to get used to putting yourself in other people's shoes to understand their perspective!

Summary

In this chapter, we have explored the fourth pillar of the C.A.R.E. Model: Evolution. We delved into the topic of evolution, focusing on elements related to personal growth and development, seeing challenges as opportunities, adapting to constant uncertainty, engaging actively, harnessing energy and pursuing excellence. We have seen how each one of us can evolve and try to enable positive change and to make a meaningful impact in the world, ultimately improving the human experience. Some of the practical tips given are designed to help your personal and professional growth and inspire you to shine your bright light into the world and have the courage to contribute to a more compassionate and innovative society. Use the skills and talents you've got to light up the darkness by resonating with a higher moral, collective purpose, and always offer a helping hand to someone in need.

Conclusion:
Key Takeaways And
Next Steps

The C.A.R.E. Model encourages you to work in synergy with your spiritual self, using the pillars of Connection to ignite your Authenticity and Re-engineer your life towards a more fulfilling and purpose-driven existence, enabling you to experience Evolution.

By taking C.A.R.E. of yourself, you are taking care of others, and if you incorporate some of the techniques explored in this book in your daily life, you will deepen your spiritual connection and find greater fulfilment in everything that surrounds you. It works for me and others, and I wrote this book to share with you this shift towards mindfulness and spiritual growth, which can truly lead you to a more balanced and harmonious existence with greater purpose and meaning. After reading the book, I invite you to make an intentional choice and truly look after yourself and connect with your inner self using the C.A.R.E. Model to guide you along the path. The advice in these pages will lead you to a sense of inner peace and contentment. The C.A.R.E. Model provokes questions about your true self, making you reflect on your values and beliefs. As it encourages you to connect with yourself on a deeper level, it will stay in your mind for a long time, and you will find yourself flashing back to some of the concepts discussed in your search for that sense of fulfilment and purpose. The model was designed to inspire people to believe in themselves and activate their power for the betterment of society, and to have the courage to act in accordance with their convictions. It works from the inside out, starting with each individual raising their consciousness by creating a deeper connection with oneself and others, rippling into organisations and our communities.

As we come to the end of this journey, let us take a moment to reflect on the insights and practical tips of the C.A.R.E. Model. This strategy, which stands for Connection, Authenticity, Re-engineering and Evolution, offers a holistic approach that can be used in both personal and professional development. It empowers you to spread your wings and make a difference in your loved ones' lives, in the lives of your team members, and the organisation you are working for, creating an empowering effect that enhances human and customer experiences globally. Truly, you can change the world by changing you.

Key lessons from the C.A.R.E. Model

Throughout this book, we have talked about how we can battle some of the issues we deal with on a daily basis, analysing the C.A.R.E. Model components and bringing them together into a holistic approach to personal growth and development. We have seen that by embracing the principles of the C.A.R.E. Model, a transformative power activates within us:

1. **Connection:** We have seen how striving to build genuine relationships and fostering a sense of community is of critical importance in our world, which is too often eroded by hatred and division. An awakened consciousness helps us nurture relationships with empathy on a more meaningful level, and maintaining a spiritual connection with God or whichever higher power you might believe in gives us an attitude of gratitude, making us mindful and improving our mental health.

2. **Authenticity:** Celebrate your uniqueness! Do not reflect the world around you, but be bold and live with originality and embrace your true self, and always align your actions with your core values. You can help bring your dreams into existence by honouring your personal values and beliefs and trusting yourself. Remember to reframe setbacks as chances to learn from experience, feed your intrinsic motivation and

find the strength to trust the process, while considering rejections as a divine redirection of your life.

3. **Re-engineering:** This component of the model focuses on the importance of adopting a success mindset and building resilience by becoming relentlessness in the face of adversity. Some of the key steps include assessing your current situation and gaining a progressive perspective to help redesign some of the processes and establish good habits. Framing crises as opportunities also helps you manage them more effectively and plan for success. We all have an in-built power to transform our lives by improving continuously and better positioning ourselves to adapt to challenges that will come our way.

4. **Evolution:** Embracing continuous growth and constant development is essential in a constantly changing world. Embracing evolution in your life allows you to shift your focus onto personal growth and transformation, grasp the challenges you face and learn to adapt to uncertainty. It is essential that you believe that harnessing your creative energy and engaging meaningfully in your pursuit of excellence will lead you to fulfilment on your journey and, ultimately, you will contribute to the enhancement of the overall human experience.

The ripple effect: Everyone CAN make a difference

The power of the C.A.R.E. Model lies in its simplicity: looking at where we are as a people and imagining a better world for us and our children. Its goal is to enable change and create ripple effects, starting with each individual and extending into the teams and organisations we work for across all industries, and out into the community as a whole. It is intended to become a spark for personal development in all parts of life.

You, me, and each of us can use our natural gifts and abilities and embrace the principles of the C.A.R.E. Model to become more conscious about our future and strive to make a positive difference in the world. We are stronger together, and we must not let ourselves be controlled by the negative forces that are in the world and overwhelm us. We can decide for ourselves and mobilise our potential to create a community of empowered individuals with a stronger sense of purpose and a moral duty to leave a lasting legacy for our children. Together, we can draw inspiration from our *why* and strive to become more resilient and motivated to attain our goals, and we can take hope in the knowledge that our efforts will have an impact for generations to come.

1. **Teams:** As each of us evolve, we contribute within our teams, which become more cohesive, supportive and inventive. Genuine connections that are built on empathy,

integrity and authenticity create trust
and a collaboration between people. Life
re-engineering and personal evolution lead
to continuous improvement and adaptability,
resulting in better performance and higher
work productivity. This gives us a feeling of
satisfaction in our job, which is essential for a
healthy organisational culture and a fulfilling
work environment.

2. **Organisations:** It is widely acknowledged
that strongly bonded teams contribute to the
overall success of their businesses, resulting
in enhanced profitability and a competitive
advantage for the organisation. Long-term
sustainability and customer loyalty have always
been the goal of organisations. Transformative
leaders who adopt the C.A.R.E. Model create
a culture of quality, innovation and inclusion,
offering an improved ability to respond swiftly
to changing market conditions and driving
innovation. Their progressive mindset puts
them in a better position to overcome obstacles,
attract and retain talented personnel and
provide excellent customer experiences. This
comprehensive approach to development
improves organisational resilience and growth.

3. **Industries:** When businesses from many
industries embrace change, the results can be
tremendous. The corporate world becomes
more dynamic, responsive, and customer-centric

as a focus on connection and authenticity develops strong customer connections, while re-engineering and evolution drive innovation and efficiency.

4. **Well-being:** If each us lives according to the power of our principles, together we can create a more harmonious world for future generations. It helps to reframe our perspective about the world, and instead of deepening the divisions between us, we should consider our differences as being great advantages that complete each other, defining who we really are as one people. It all starts with the power of each one of us being willing to put in the hard work; we should feel encouraged to inspire positive change and build a better world for all, living with kindness and compassion.

Businesses that prioritise human and customer experiences set new benchmarks for excellence. This creates a positive feedback loop where exceptional customer experiences drive brand loyalty and market growth, and the more industries adopt these principles, the more the global market becomes more integrated and human experience-focused. Prioritising empathy and understanding in all our interactions, as well as putting ourselves in the shoes of our customers and validating their wants and needs, is how *we transform the customer experience.* We should always treat others how we want to be treated, and remember that if we actively listen and respond with empathy, we arrive at a deeper understanding and connection with our customers while providing a more meaningful customer experience.

Summary

The C.A.R.E. Model emphasises the importance of a transformed human experience in designing exceptional customer experiences. When people and organisations embrace these principles, a better understanding of the customers' needs is achieved:

- **Enhanced customer experience:** Genuine connections and empathy determine a deeper understanding of customer preferences, promoting a more personalised and improved service.

- **Innovation:** Re-engineering processes drive continuous innovation on the road to evolution. With this approach in mind, products and services may be enhanced to meet and exceed changing customer demands.

- **Stronger relationships:** Authenticity and genuine engagement builds trust and fosters long-term relationships.

- **Global excellence:** These principles are not limited only to a few industries, but have a wide applicability as the standard of customer experience rises globally and setting new benchmarks for service and the quality of human interconnections becomes essential.

Next steps: Start implementing the C.A.R.E. Model today

We have been talking for some time about making a difference, and now is the right time to act and begin using the C.A.R.E. Model in your everyday life to attain the state of well-being you desire and to help build more positive communities. Whether you are someone seeking personal development, a manager wishing for team cohesion or an organisation looking to improve your team performance or enhance your customers' experience, the C.A.R.E. Model gives you the tools to succeed. Around the C.A.R.E. Model described in this book, a more complex strategy can be designed for individuals and organisations committed to upgrading their lives or transforming their teams to achieve thriving and sustainable development. My courses and individual mentoring programmes complement the C.A.R.E. Model by providing in-depth, effective techniques that are designed to attain a deep level of introspection and identify areas for improvement along with actionable steps to implement positive change.

If you feel you need additional assistance with the implementation or wish to have personalised guidance, I am here for you. I will commit my time to assisting you or your team in successfully incorporating the C.A.R.E.

Model into your everyday routines or operations. If you represent an organisation, together we will develop a tailored strategy that better suits the organisation's goals. We will design the process to enhance the customer experience and work towards the organisational development. If you are a person who simply wants more from your life, we can work together towards personal development. In our individual mentoring sessions, I can guide you to enhance the state of your well-being and how to work relentlessly to achieve your boldest dreams.

If you would like to discuss more about how I can support you on your journey, feel free to contact me directly by e-mail: office@ghleaders.com. If you are looking for additional materials to study at your own pace from the comfort of your home, you can access my specialised courses on my website www.ghleaders.com or simply scan the QR code to reserve your spot today on any course or coaching session. This is designed to help you dive deeper into the C.A.R.E. Model, gain personalised insights and develop effective strategies for achieving your maximum potential.

I hope you have enjoyed reading this book and I look forward to getting to know you and guide you along your journey. Remember, if you can dream it, you can achieve it! So, Dare to C.A.R.E. and let's get to work! Let's embrace the advanced C.A.R.E. Master Programme and enhance the human experience. Thank you for your time. God bless you.

References

Amabile, TM, *Creativity in Context* (Westview Press, 1996)

Argyris, C, 'Teaching smart people how to learn', *Harvard Business Review*, 69/3 (1991), 99–109

Covey, SR, *The 7 Habits of Highly Effective People* (Free Press, 1989)

Craik, FIM and Bialystok, E, 'Cognition through the lifespan: Mechanisms of change', *Trends in Cognitive Sciences*, 10/3 (2006), 131–138

Deci, EL and Ryan, RM, 'The "what" and "why" of goal pursuits: Human needs and the self-determination of behavior', *Psychological Inquiry*, 11/4 (2000), 227–268

Dweck, CS, *Mindset: The new psychology of success* (Random House, 2006)

Emmons, RA and McCullough, ME, 'Counting blessings versus burdens: An experimental investigation of gratitude and subjective well-being in daily life', *Journal of Personality and Social Psychology*, 84/2 (2003), 377–389

Fader, P and Toms, S, *The Customer Centricity Playbook* (Wharton Digital Press, 2018)

Frankl, VE, *Man's Search for Meaning* (Beacon Press, 2006)

Goleman, D, *Emotional Intelligence: Why it can matter more than IQ* (Bantam Books, 1995)

Goleman, D, Boyatzis, R and McKee A, *Primal Leadership: Unleashing the power of emotional intelligence* (Harvard Business Review Press, 2013)

Guzzo, RA, Fink, AA, King, E, Tonidandel, S and Landis, RS, 'The future of research methods in diversity management: Lessons from industrial and organisational psychology', *Human Resource Management*, 53/2 (2014), 203–214

Hammer, M and Champy, J, *Re-engineering the Corporation: Manifesto for business revolution* (Harper Business, 2009)

Hofstede, G, *Culture's Consequences: Comparing values, behaviours, institutions, and organisations across nations* (Sage Publications, 2001)

Humphrey, A, *SWOT Analysis for Management Consulting* (SRI Alumni Association Newsletter, 2005)

Isaacson, W, *Benjamin Franklin: An American life* (Simon & Schuster, 2003)

Kabat-Zinn, J, *Full Catastrophe Living: Using the wisdom of your body and mind to face stress, pain, and illness* (Delacorte, 1990)

Kabat-Zinn, J, *Wherever You Go, There You Are: Mindfulness meditation in everyday life* (Hyperion, 1994)

Kaplan, RS and Norton, DP, *The Balanced Scorecard: Translating strategy into action* (Harvard Business Review Press, 1996)

Kelley, K, *Oprah: A biography* (Crown, 2011)

Kolb, DA, *Experiential Learning: Experience as the source of learning and development* (Prentice-Hall, 1984)

Kouzes, JM and Posner, BZ, *The Leadership Challenge* (Jossey-Bass, 2007)

Lencioni, P, *The Five Dysfunctions of a Team: A leadership fable* (Jossey-Bass, 2002)

Locke, EA and Latham, GP, 'Building a practically useful theory of goal setting and task motivation: A

35-year odyssey', *American Psychologist*, 57/9 (2002), 705–717

Louv, R, *Last Child in the Woods: Saving our children from nature-deficit disorder* (Algonquin Books, 2008)

Mediratta, B, *The Google Way: Give engineers room* (The New York Times, 2007)

Northouse, PG, *Leadership: Theory and practice* (Sage Publications, 2018)

Parks, R and Haskins, J, *Rosa Parks: My story* (Dial Books, 1992)

Pine II, B and Gilmore, J, 'The experience economy: past, present and future'. In: Sundbo, J and Sørensen, F (eds), *Handbook on the Experience Economy* (Edward Elgar Publishing, 2013)

Robinson, D, Perryman, S and Hayday, S, *The Drivers of Employee Engagement* (Institute for Employment Studies, 2004)

Robinson, K, *Out of Our Minds: Learning to be creative* (Capstone, 2011)

Rowling, JK, *Very Good Lives: The fringe benefits of failure and the importance of imagination* (Little, Brown and Company, 2015)

Schein, EH, *Organisational Culture and Leadership* (Jossey-Bass, 2010)

Senge, PM, *The Fifth Discipline: The art & practice of the learning organisation* (Doubleday, 2006)

Spreitzer, GM, 'Psychological empowerment in the workplace: Dimensions, measurement, and validation', *Academy of Management Journal*, 38/5 (1995), 1442–1465

Tuckman, BW, 'Developmental sequence in small groups', *Psychological Bulletin*, 63/6 (1965), 384–399

Twenge, JM, *iGen: Why today's super-connected kids are growing up less rebellious, more tolerant, less happy – and completely unprepared for adulthood* (Atria Books, 2017)

Vance, A, *Elon Musk: Tesla, SpaceX, and the quest for a fantastic future* (Ecco, 2015)

Vlasceanu, CF and Țigu, G, 'Resilience and recovery: The impact of Covid-19 pandemic on the global cruise tourism'. In: Dima, AM and Kelemen M (eds), *Digitalization and Big Data for Resilience and Economic Intelligence* (pp. 245–258), (Springer, 2021)

Vlasceanu, CF, *Re-engineering business models centred on customer experience and innovative approach to service excellence in cruising industry* [dissertation], Bucharest University of Economic Studies (2024)

World Health Organization (WHO), *Global Recommendations on Physical Activity for Health* (WHO Press, 2010)

Yousafzai, M, *I Am Malala: The girl who stood up for education and was shot by the Taliban* (Little, Brown and Company, 2013)

Ziglar, Z, *See You at the Top* (Pelican Publishing, 1997)

Further Information

I have put together a list of books and resources for you, providing you with comprehensive materials that will further inspire you to live an authentic, resilient and excellent life, while also leading and inspiring your loved ones to enhance the human experience for the greater good. These resources cover a wide range of topics and perspectives, providing you with valuable insights on authenticity, resilience, excellence, leadership and the broader human experience.

Berger, J, *Invisible Influence: The hidden forces that shape behaviour* (Simon & Schuster, 2017)

Brown, B, *The Power of Vulnerability* (Sounds True, 2013)

Brown, B, *Dare to Lead: Brave work. Tough conversations. Whole hearts*, by Brené Brown (Random House, 2018)

Brown, B, *The Gifts of Imperfection: Let go of who you think you're supposed to be and embrace who you are* (Hazelden FIRM, 2018)

Cain, S, *Quiet: The power of introverts in a world that can't stop talking* (Penguin, 2013)

Canfield, J and Switzer, J, *The Success Principles: How to get from where you are to where you want to be* (William Morrow Paperbacks, 2015)

Carr, N, *The Glass Cage: How our computers are changing us* (WW Norton & Company, 2015)

Carr, N, *The Shallows: What the internet is doing to our brains* (WW Norton & Company, 2011)

Carter, J, *A Call to Action: Women, religion, violence, and power* (Simon & Schuster, 2014)

Cialdini, RB, *Influence: The psychology of persuasion* (HarperBus, 2007)

Clear, J, *Atomic Habits: An easy & proven way to build good habits & break bad ones* (Avery, 2018)

Compernolle, T, *Brain Chains: Discover your brain and unleash its full potential in a hyperconnected multitasking world* (Compublications, 2014)

Davenport, TH and Beck, JC, *The Attention Economy: Understanding the new currency of business* (Harvard Business Review, 2001)

David, S, *Emotional Agility: Get unstuck, embrace change, and thrive in work and life* (Penguin Life, 2016)

de Zengotita, T, *Mediated: How the media shapes your world and the way you live in it* (Bloomsbury, 2006)

Doyle, G, *Untamed* (Ebury Publishing, 2020)

Duckworth, A, *Grit: The power of passion and perseverance* (Scribner Book Company, 2016)

Duhigg, C, *The Power of Habit: Why we do what we do in life and business* (Random House, 2014)

Dweck, CS, *Mindset: The new psychology of success* (Random House, 2007)

Eyal, N, *Hooked: How to build habit-forming products* (Portfolio, 2014)

Frankl, VE, *Man's Search for Meaning* (Beacon Press, 2006)

García Martínez, A, *Chaos Monkeys: Obscene fortune and random failure in Silicon Valley* (HarperCollins, 2016)

Gazzaley, A and Rosen, LD, *The Distracted Mind: Ancient brains in a high-tech world* (MIT Press, 2016)

George, B, *True North: Discover your authentic leadership* (John Wiley & Sons, 2007)

Goldsmith, M, *What Got You Here Won't Get You There: How successful people become even more successful* (Profile Books, 2008)

Goodwin, DK, *Leadership in Turbulent Times* (Simon & Schuster, 2018)

Grant, A, *Originals: How non-conformists move the world* (Viking, 2016)

Hanson, R, *Resilient: How to grow an unshakable core of calm, strength, and happiness* (Random House, 2018)

Herman, ES and Chomsky, N, *Man's Search for Meaning, Manufacturing Consent: The political economy of the mass media* (Vintage, 1995)

Hindman, M, *The Internet Trap: How the digital economy builds monopolies and undermines democracy* (Princeton University Press, 2018)

Holiday, R, *The Obstacle Is the Way: The timeless art of turning trials into triumph* (Portfolio, 2014)

Hollis, J, *Why Good People Do Bad Things: Understanding our darker selves* (Penguin, 2008)

Huffington, A, *Thrive: The third metric to redefining success and creating a life of well-being, wisdom, and wonder* (Harmony, 2015)

Kishimi, I and Koga, F, *The Courage to Be Disliked: How to free yourself, change your life, and achieve real happiness* (Allen & Unwin, 2018)

Lanier, J, *You Are Not a Gadget: A manifesto* (Penguin, 2011)

Lencioni, P, *The Five Dysfunctions of a Team: A leadership fable* (Jossey-Bass, 2002)

Levitin, DJ, *The Organized Mind: Thinking straight in the age of information overload* (Dutton, 2015)

McKeown, G, *Essentialism: The disciplined pursuit of less* (Virgin Books, 2014)

Menn, J, *Cult of the Dead Cow: How the original hacking supergroup might just save the world* (Public Affairs, 2019)

Newport, C, *Deep Work: Rules for focused success in a distracted world* (Piatkus, 2016)

Newport, C, *Digital Minimalism: Choosing a focused life in a noisy world* (Portfolio Penguin, 2019)

Noble, SU, *Algorithms of Oppression: How search engines reinforce racism* (NYU Press, 2018)

O'Neil, C, *Weapons of Math Destruction: How big data increases inequality and threatens democracy* (Crown Publishing Group, 2016)

Obama, M, *Becoming* (Viking, 2018)

Parisier, E, *The Filter Bubble: How the new personalized web is changing what we read and how we think* (Penguin, 2012)

Pink, DH, *Drive: The surprising truth about what motivates us* (Cannongate Books, 2011)

Postman, N, *Amusing Ourselves to Death: Public discourse in the age of show business* (Methuen Publishing, 1985)

Pressfield, S, *The War of Art: Break through the blocks and win your inner creative battles* (Black Irish Entertainment, 2012)

Ronson, J, *So You've Been Publicly Shamed* (Riverhead Books, 2015)

Rosling, H, *Factfulness: Ten reasons we're wrong about the world – and why things are better than you think* (Sceptre, 2018)

Sandberg, S, *Lean In: Women, work, and the will to lead* (WH Allen, 2013)

Scott, K, *Radical Candor: Be a kick-ass boss without losing your humanity* (St Martins, 2017)

Sincero, J, *You Are a Badass: How to stop doubting your greatness and start living an awesome life* (Running Press Adult, 2013)

Sinek, S, *Start with Why: How great leaders inspire everyone to take action* (Penguin, 2011)

Taleb, NN, *Antifragile: Things that gain from disorder* (Penguin, 2012)

Thaler, RH and Sunstein, CR, *Nudge: Improving decisions about health, wealth, and happiness* (Penguin, 2009)

Tolle, E, *The Power of Now: A guide to spiritual enlightenment* (Yellow Kite, 2001)

Turkle, S, *Reclaiming Conversation: The power of talk in a digital age* (Penguin, 2016)

Walker, M, *Why We Sleep: Unlocking the power of sleep and dreams* (Simon & Schuster, 2017)

Wu, T, *The Attention Merchants: The epic scramble to get inside our heads* (Alfred A Knopf, 2016)

Zander, RS and Zander, B, *The Art of Possibility: Transforming professional and personal life* (Harvard Business Review, 2000)

Zuboff, S, *The Age of Surveillance Capitalism: The fight for a human future at the new frontier of power* (Profile Books, 2019)

Acknowledgements

My deepest gratitude goes to my family, Adam, Mum, Dad, my sister Daniela, my beautiful niece Bianca-Gabriela, and Bailey. I am very appreciative of your genuine love and comfort in trying times, and for being there for me, especially when undertaking such a daring project seemed so surreal to me. I'd like to thank my dear friends Maria, Ramona, Amira, for their encouragements and prayers. My guiding professor and my role model, Prof Univ. Dr. Gabriela Țigu, Dean of the Faculty of Business and Tourism at the Bucharest University of Economic Studies. Thank you for sharing with me your knowledge, experience and passion for the tourism industry. Your enthusiasm and optimism kept me going ahead with my academic research, and I consider myself fortunate to have had you as my thesis coordinator and guiding mentor throughout the doctoral programme.

My heartfelt gratitude also goes to the industry leaders, entrepreneurs, mentors, and academics. Your encouragement has been the wind beneath my wings, enabling me to reach new heights.

To my worldwide hospitality network, your collective wisdom gave me the motivation to write and share my insights into the amazing world of hospitality.

I also extend my sincere thanks to my colleagues and my global network in the cruise community, and to the Institute of Hospitality, for inspiring me along the way to advance my knowledge and contribute to the existing scientific literature. I am looking forward to our ongoing and successful relationship, and together we will contribute to the progress of the cruise hospitality and global tourism sectors.

Thank you to everyone who played a part, whether in the classroom, boardroom, or out on the blue oceans. This book exemplifies humanity's collaborative spirit, bringing together shared experiences and collective wisdom. May its pages evoke a spirit of thankfulness and encourage others on their own life journeys.

With heartfelt appreciation,

Carmen F. Vlasceanu PhD, MBA, FIH

The Author

With over twenty-five years of hospitality experience, Carmen started her career studying the hotel industry and working as an intern in various hotels, as well as in the Alfa Rocas Airline Catering company, at the international airport in Bucharest, Romania. Around the same time, she was a regular correspondent for a local food and beverage magazine, where she wrote monthly articles.

Carmen's life journey opened the possibilities of travelling the world when she joined Carnival Cruise Lines, working aboard many beautiful cruise ships.

For the following eleven years, Carmen developed her career in the purser department as one of the officers on board, working up through the ranks. Her five-star experience in hospitality was rewarded by being promoted to Chief Purser/Guest Services Manager, in charge of the guest services department, responsible for the well-being of over 5,000 guests and their exceptional cruise hospitality experience aboard the majestic floating hotels.

After over a decade of working and travelling the world's oceans and visiting amazing exotic ports, she returned to Bucharest where she had her son Adam, and soon after she undertook studies to elevate her academic achievement to the same level as her professional expertise. She finished a master's in Hotel Revenue Management at Cornell University of Management Studies in New York, and went on to earn a bachelor's degree in Management and Marketing at the Romanian-American University in Bucharest, graduating as a valedictorian. She undertook specialised certification programmes and received her certification as Hotel Director and Tourism Manager awarded by the National Ministry. Carmen then underwent an MBA in Entrepreneurship and International Business at the Romanian-American University, while working for Travco Corporation UK.

During the academic tenure, as a single mum, Carmen worked at the US Department of State based in Bucharest, coordinating the students' US Summer Work and Travel Program, while participating in many extracurricular courses, workshops and business conferences. In 2008, she joined the Institute of Hospitality and was awarded Fellow status (FIH) in recognition of her professional expertise, and was designated as the Institute's exclusive Ambassador to the Romanian market. Carmen co-founded a travel agency where she was Managing Director, while continuing to study to further her academic endeavor.

The life journey has exposed her to a myriad of experiences, and over the years she joined forces with numerous organisations hosting events for the InterNations global expat community and a member of the Harvard Business Review Advisory Council opt-in research business professionals community. Unfortunately, the events of the global pandemic forced her travel agency to close, but continuing to study, she wrote and published a number of scientific articles and was a speaker at international conferences.

Carmen joined a company based in the UK working as an MD. She graduated, magna cum laude, with a PhD in Business Administration, Cruise and Global Hospitality. Her PhD research area was centred on Customer Experience and the successful recovery of the cruise industry amid the uncertainties of the Covid-19 pandemic.

Throughout her career, Carmen has been passionate about developing aspiring managers, and she has undergone specialised training programmes and received her certification as a personal development life coach. As a mentor, she is currently working closely with clients in one-to-one counselling sessions or group settings within business organisations, dedicating herself to training and developing their human talent. Being passionate about creating positive effects that will ripple out into the world and make a difference, she founded Angels-Wings.org, a nonprofit organisation whose goal is to inspire people and to help with food, clothes and education for children and people that are less fortunate in life. As actions speak louder than words, Carmen proved to be a relentless advocate for personal development, equality and education, and wrote this book *Dare to C.A.R.E.* to raise awareness, encourage people and actively contribute to the well-being of our society and enhance the human experience.

🌐 www.ghleaders.com

🌐 Angels-Wings.org